TOGETHER:
Devotions for
Young Children and Families

TOGETHER:
Devotions for
Young Children and Families

Trudy Pettibone

CONQUEST
PUBLISHERS

Bladensburg, Maryland

Conquest Publishers
A division of Conquest Industries LLC
P.O. Box 611
Bladensburg, MD 20710-0611
www.conquestpublishers.com

ISBN 10: 0-9656625-9-4
ISBN 13: 978-0-9656625-9-8

Library of Congress Control Number: 2012943017
Printed in the United States of America

Scriptures used in memory verses for children have been modified for simplicity and to enhance readability for younger children.

Dedication

To the children of the year 2000 two and three-year-old Sunday School Class and their families of the Lakewood Baptist Church in Cincinnati, Ohio, who showed me the benefit of devotions like these. Thank you.

Contents

Old Testament

1. A Week of Creation

2. Early Ancestors

3. The Lord Starts a New Family

4. Abraham's Family Goes to Egypt

5. Abraham's Family Leaves Egypt

6. Israelites in the Wilderness

10. The People in a Strange Land

New Testament

1. The Messiah

2. Jesus Begins His Ministry

3. Teachings and Examples

4. Miracles of Jesus

5. Jesus' Last Days

6. The Beginning of a New Church

7. Paul's Missionary Travels

8. Special Teachings

Preface

These devotions are designed as resources to help parents teach their children about the Lord. I believe that spiritual growth happens at home as well as at church, and that children are never too young to learn about spiritual matters.

These devotions are intended mainly for families with children from toddlers to 2nd grade. If there are older children, they might help read, ask questions or help with the activities. The whole family should be included as much as possible.

Each devotional includes the following:

- a scripture passage

- a verse or words for memory for both older and younger children

- a brief meditation, denoted by the   symbol.

- a prayer, denoted by the   symbol.

- suggested discussion points, denoted by the   symbol.

- suggested activities, preceded by the   symbol.

The meditations are designed for the adults or older children, to provide some additional "thought" material for leading the younger children. Meditations will offer suggestions for the goal of the devotion.

The memory verse is to be adapted according to the age of the children. A shorter version for younger children is directly below the memory verse. Sometimes, the verse will be too long for memory, but should be given special focus. The discussion questions and activities are suggestions, and should be modified according to the child's interests and age. The discussion questions are designed to get the child's imaginative juices flowing and thinking about the subject, not to provide definitive or correct answers.

Unless otherwise indicated, Scriptures are taken from the New Revised Standard Version Bible. The use of a bible geared to a child's understanding might be helpful for reading the scripture passages. Don't hesitate to use other books, e.g., history, science or picture books, to help the child understand some of the more difficult concepts. Be sure to relate to the child on his/her educational and social level in trying to help the child understand.

You will notice that the gender-specific pronouns, such as "him" and "her," in referring to children, change from one devotion to the other. This is done to give the devotions a feel of inclusivity. Use of a gender-specific pronoun should not be interpreted to mean that the activity is meant only for that specific gender.

Old Testament

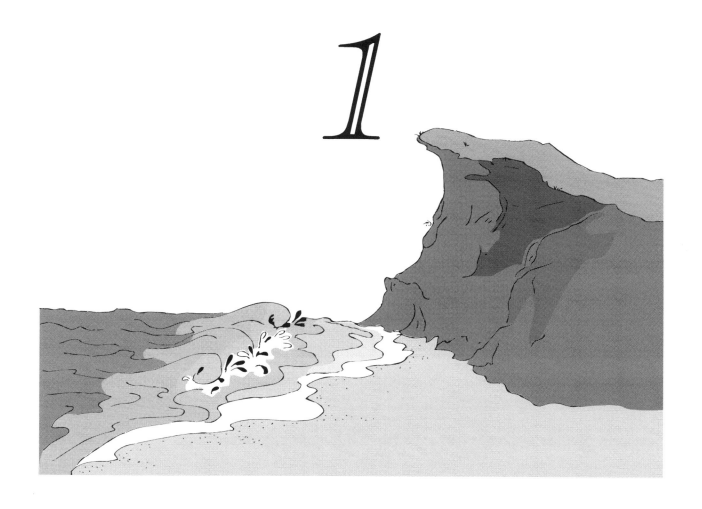

A Week of Creation

Day One: God Creates Light

Scripture: Genesis 1:1-5 (NIV)

Memory: Genesis 1:1
In the beginning God created the heavens and the earth.

Memory verse for younger children:
God created the heavens and the earth.

 **Meditation** It took several years of reading this passage before I discovered something that put my understanding of sun and moon into question. Day and night happened before the sun and moon were created. Light came into existence without these two governing bodies. God spoke, and light happened.

We are told that Jesus is the light of the world (John 8:12), but Jesus wasn't created. Jesus was always with God. When God spoke, Jesus was there, because Jesus is also the Word (John 1:1). What is this light that came to be in the midst of the vast darkness and was separated from the darkness? Some might think that this was the "big bang," a cosmic explosion of light that started the formation of the earth.

God took formless darkness, and created our earth. He gave it form and shape, and he made night and day. Then, God said it was good. Everything that God made was good. Throughout these days of creation, help the child understand that God's creation is good.

Prayer: Thank you God that you created the earth. Thank you for making light, which lights our ways. Amen.

 For Discussion: Ask the child what the light might have been. Talk about God speaking the light into being. Ask the child to describe what the earth may have looked like before God made light.

Activity: Shine a flashlight in a dark room, and help the child understand how it overcomes the darkness. (2) Have the child draw a picture of the formless void before God created light. (3) If the child is afraid of the dark, talk about how light helps the child not be afraid.

NOTES

Day Two: God Makes the Sky

Scripture: Genesis 1:6-8

Memory: Genesis 1:8
God called the dome Sky. And there was evening and there was morning, the second day.

Memory verse for younger children:
God called the dome Sky.

 **Meditation:** In the ancient world, the earth was seen as a dome, and the creation story follows this idea. God made the dome, or expanse, which God called "sky." It had water above and below. God separated these two groups of water, but we still have no land. The earth at this point is a watery mass, with two parts separated by the sky.

God may not have spoken this expanse into existence. God said "let there be," but then we are told that "God made the expanse." We will see God making several other things in this creation story. When God made the dome, God named it. Help the child understand that everything God created was given special thought and was created for a particular purpose. God cared enough about what was made to give them names.

 Prayer: Thank you Lord that you made the sky. Help me understand how there was water without land. Amen.

For discussion: Help the child understand this idea of a watery mass, with a "dome" separating two masses of water, but no land. Ask the child how he might have created the world. Ask the child how she thinks God might have made the dome.

Activity: This is such a difficult concept to understand, it might just be best to allow the child to create, using different materials, like dough, cotton, slime or other things to demonstrate the child's understanding of this second day.

NOTES

Day Three: God Makes Land, Seas and Plants

Scripture: Genesis 1:9-13

Memory: Genesis 1:10
God called the dry land Earth, and the waters that were gathered together he called Seas. And God saw that it was good.

Memory verse for younger children:
God called the dry land Earth, and the waters he called Seas.

Meditation: In the creation story, we don't hear about the waters above the dome anymore. Now the earth begins to look familiar to us, except for one thing: all the water is in one place. This is not really hard to imagine if we look at a globe. Some continents seem like they really could fit right up against others. This land "appeared" when God gathered all the waters together. It is interesting that the gathered waters are called "seas" not "sea."

Then we see vegetation appearing at the spoken word of God. A law of nature is instilled within these fruits and vegetables: they will produce seed according to their own kind. This means that pumpkins will not produce grape seed, and apple trees will not produce apricots. It is only with modern science that we see hybrids created from two or more different types of plants.

The child should understand that God created variety not just because it was pleasing to the eye, but because God was planning to create people, and knew that they would appreciate the variety.

 Prayer: God, thank you that you created fruits and vegetables for us to enjoy, and seas for the earth. Amen.

For Discussion: Ask the child what fruits or vegetables God may have created first, or if they were all created at once. How many fruits and vegetables do you think God made? Talk about how the land may have appeared when the waters were gathered together. Using an appropriate book, talk about volcanoes that erupt and make new land. Talk about what it might be like if all the continents were joined together (e.g., ships might not have been invented).

Activity: (1) Look at a globe or map and point out to the child how the continents may at one time been joined together. Talk about what may have caused them to separate. (2) Have the child talk about his favorite fruit and vegetables, and draw pictures of them. (3) On a trip to the grocery story, point out fruits and vegetables which are unfamiliar to the child. (4) Help the child find new recipes for fruits and vegetables and make a simple dish for the family.

NOTES

Day Four: God Makes the Sun, Moon and Stars

Scripture: Genesis 1:14-19

Memory: Genesis 1:14
And God said, "Let there be lights in the dome of the sky to separate the day from the night; and let them be for signs and for seasons and for days and years."

Memory verse for younger children:
And God said, "Let there be lights in the dome of the sky."

Meditation: Notice that God does not give names to these two great lights in the sky. They are designed to separate day from night, and to be markers for the seasons, days and years.

The most simplistic statement in this passage concerns the creation of the stars, verse 16. One might get the impression of lights being merely sprinkled across the heavens. We certainly do not see uncountable numbers of planets, many of which are larger than our own planet or even our sun. This text is written within the understanding of its author, who truly only knew the stars as little twinkling lights up in the sky. The moon and stars came to light the sky at night, and the "great ball" to light the day. Help the child understand how the sun and moon relate to our seasons and days.

Prayer: God, thank you for the sun that gives us warmth and light in the day, and the moon and stars that light our way at night.

Amen.

 For Discussion: Talk about the order of creation up to this point. Ask the child why she thinks God created plants, which need sun, before God created the sun. Help the child understand how the sun relates to the change in seasons.

Activity: (1) Go to a planetarium and look at the moon and stars at night, or sit outside and watch them several nights in a row. Identify certain things, e.g., the moon, and talk about how they are in different places. (2) Help the child make a simple mobile of the earth, its sun and moon.

NOTES

Day Five: God Creates Fish and Birds

Scripture: Genesis 1:20-23

Memory: Genesis 1:20
And God said, "Let the waters bring forth swarms of living creatures, and let birds fly above the earth across the dome of the sky."

Memory verse for younger children:
"Let the waters bring forth swarms of living creatures, and let birds fly above the earth."

Meditation: In describing the creatures of the sea, some translations actually use the term "sea monsters," including the NRSV. This might disturb some children. There are gigantic creatures in the sea, some of which we may not even know about yet. Like the vegetation, these creatures reproduce according to their kind. Something new is added here: God speaks to these creatures. God blesses them and commands them to be fruitful and increase. God speaks to his creation as if it had comprehension, and it may have had. In Isaiah 55:12, we see trees clapping their hands. There may be many things in God's creation which are foreign to us, things we may consider impossible, but with God all things are possible. Creation before the bondage of sin may be something we cannot begin to imagine. Help the child understand that many things may exist that we don't understand, but with a child's imagination, this probably won't be a problem.

Prayer: Thank you God for all the fish of the sea and the birds of the sky. Amen.

 For Discussion: If the child is not intimidated by the idea of "monsters," talk about what monsters might be in the ocean. Ask the child why he thinks God created fish and birds together. Talk about the idea of God talking to the birds and fish.

 Activity: (1) Look at picture books of birds and fish. (2) Have the child imagine what they might say if they could talk to fish or birds.

NOTES

Day Six: God Creates Land Animals and God Creates Me

Scripture: Genesis 1:24-31

Memory: Genesis 1:24
And God said, "Let the earth bring forth living creatures of every kind:
cattle and creeping things and wild animals of the earth of every kind."
And it was so.

Memory verse for younger children:
And God said, "Let the earth bring forth living creatures of every kind."

Meditation: On this last day of creation, we see that God creates the "big" things that would roam the earth, including humanity. Again, they are produced, and will reproduce, according to their kind. God also created the animals that move along the ground, like the serpent that we will meet a little later. Guess what we don't see created at this time? Insects. Nothing is said about teeming creatures on the earth, or teeming creatures in the sky.

All creation is in place now, so it is time for God to create the jewel of creation, and the caretaker of the creation: humanity. This segment of Genesis tells us that God created male and female. The specific details come in chapter two. God gave these creatures the privilege of eating from almost every plant, and gave the same privilege to all the other animals. There is no idea of humans eating meat, or of animals eating one another. These things will all come later. For now, God looked at all of creation and found it to be good. The child will want to know that he is especially created by God, with gifts and talents to be used for God.

Prayer: Thank you God that you made animals that could be my pets, and that you created me to be just like you wanted me to be. Amen.

For Discussion: If the child has a pet, talk about what it may have looked like long ago. Look at Genesis 2, verses 7, 21 and 22, which give the details of creation of the man and woman. Help the child understand how God made the man and woman. God formed them. God did not speak them into being.

 Activity: (1) With a piece of clay, help the child form a man and a woman. What names would the child give to these? (2) Encourage the child to name every animal he knows, and to make that animal's sound. (3) Help the child identify her own special characteristics, and to thank God for these.

NOTES

Day Seven: The Creator Rests

Scripture: Genesis 2:1-3

Memory: Genesis 2:2
And on the seventh day God finished the work that he had done, and he rested on the seventh day from all the work that he had done.

Memory verse for younger children:
God rested on the seventh day.

Meditation: We really underestimate this little passage, until the later development of the Ten Commandments. Then we see how important rest was to God. If rest was important to God, shouldn't it be also to us? The word "Sabbath" means to rest, cease, desist. It is used as a verb in this passage, not a noun. Later, the last day of the week, Saturday, became the Sabbath, beginning at sundown on Friday. For most Christians, the first day of the week, Sunday, became the Lord's Day. Sunday has never been the Sabbath, but it can be a day of rest and worship. God blessed the Sabbath, making it a holy day. If you have not already, begin now to encourage the child to make time for rest, stressing that rest helps us to be the best we can be for God.

In John 5:17, responding to attitudes toward Jesus' work on the Sabbath, Jesus said that his Father is still working and he is still working. Jesus emphasized that the Sabbath was made for man, and not man for the Sabbath (Mark 2:27). Rest is necessary, but not to the point of forgetting the needs of others.

Prayer: Thank you God for showing us how important rest is to you. Help us always find time to rest and worship you. Amen.

For Discussion: Why do you think God rested? Help the child understand how important rest is for us. God made the rest day a holy day. What holy day does the child observe? Talk about the ways in which your family observes holy days and rest days.

Activity: (1) If you are part of a faith community, talk about the ways in which this community recognizes their holy day. (2) Go to the building where you meet, and look at the things which are part of your holy days. (3) Ask the leader of your faith community to talk to the child about how they use their day of rest.

NOTES

Early Ancestors

Adam and Eve in the Garden

Scripture: Genesis 2:15-25

Memory: Genesis 2:18
Then the LORD God said, "It is not good that the man should be alone; I will make him a helper as his partner."

Memory verse for younger children:
"It is not good that the man should be alone."

Meditation: After God formed the man, he made a companion for him. More details of this are in Genesis chapter two. God placed the man in the garden before the woman was created, so the woman was not there when God made the rule that the man was not to eat of the tree in the middle of the garden.

God provided everything this couple needed: a beautiful place to live, all the organic fruits and vegetables they could eat, and companionship and rules. God knows that we need rules. God even gave the man a job: he was to till the garden and keep it. Sometimes we take pleasant occupation for granted. The man and woman were to care for all the animals and the plants. The first job was gardening, which was quickly followed by animal husbandry. Prior to the entry of sin into the world, these jobs might have been much easier than they are now. Help the child understand that God provided everything that this couple needed, including companionship with himself, something we don't get to experience in the same intimate way anymore.

Prayer: Dear God, thank you for all the wonderful things you give us. Please help us appreciate all these things. Amen.

 For Discussion: Talk about how beautiful this first garden must have been, and how delicious the fresh food must have been. Help the child understand that the life these people had at this time was very different from any life we have now, because they had no sin. The beauty of the garden, the taste of the food, the air around them, everything was good, because it was as God created it.

Activity: (1) Help the child make some artistic expression of what he thinks the garden might look like. (2) Visit an art museum where the child might see some art work depicting this garden.

NOTES

Adam and Eve Disobey

Scripture: Genesis 3:1-7

Memory: Genesis 3:6
So when the woman saw that the tree was good for food, and that it was a delight to the eyes, and that the tree was to be desired to make one wise, she took of its fruit and ate; and she also gave some to her husband, who was with her, and he ate.

Memory verse for younger children:
She took of its fruit and ate; and she also gave some to her husband.

Meditation: The serpent waited until the woman was alone to put his plan to work. We are always more vulnerable when we are by ourselves. The woman probably had not previously given the tree a second thought. The serpent knew all the right buttons to push. She did the wrong thing, and then quickly persuaded her husband to follow her. People are often persuaded to do wrong by those they want to please.

The man and woman did not die, as we think of death, but they died in the sense that they became separated from God. Everything was changed. God did not turn away from this couple. They had to leave the garden, but God provided for them. And God gave them a promise. One day God would provide a way for humanity to be brought back into relationship with the Divine. As Christians, we believe Jesus is that way. Jesus is the ultimate sign of God's love. Share with the child this wonderful way in which God shows his love for us, even when we do wrong.

 Prayer: Thank you, Lord, that you love me so much. Thank you that you even love me when I do wrong things. Amen.

For Discussion: Any child old enough to share this time will understand what it means to do wrong things at times. Help the child to understand that there is nothing he can do that is so terrible to make God stop loving him. Help the child recognize some of the wrong things the child has done.

Activity: (1) Have the child draw a picture of the serpent that tempted the woman; (2) Encourage the child to confess any wrongdoing to God in writing. If the child can't write, write it out for him as he dictates.

NOTES

Two Brothers Fight

Scripture: Genesis 4:1-8

Memory: Genesis 4:8
Cain said to his brother Abel, "Let us go out to the field." And when they were in the field, Cain rose up against his brother Abel, and killed him.

Memory verse for younger children:
Cain rose up against his brother Abel.

Meditation: No matter what sibling rivalry exists with your children, chances are small that one will kill the other. You may certainly see significant fights. That is the nature of brothers and sisters, and it started with these first two children born under sin. While some disagreement may be normal, ugliness and hatred are not normal and should never be accepted.

The basis of this disagreement was that God accepted the gifts of one and rejected the gifts of the other. We can't explain this. We don't know the attitudes with which the gifts were offered, or the quality of the gifts. The supposition of some that God accepted the meat but not the vegetation does not hold up, because when offerings and sacrifices are formally established, they include both grain and meat. For God's own reasons, one gift was chosen over the other, and this led to the fatal disagreement. Do your children think you favor one over the other? Help them understand that while fighting is natural, you love them equally and so does God, even when they fight.

Prayer: Precious Lord, sometimes I fight, and I know that is wrong. Help me never be nasty or mean. Amen.

For Discussion: Try to help the child discover some of the reasons why she fights, whether with a sibling, a friend, or other relative. Help the child understand that the problem between these two brothers was that God accepted Abel's gifts and rejected Cain's gifts. Be sure the child understands that God does not reject anyone who loves him. Help the child understand jealousy.

Activity: (1) Encourage the child to develop an apology for a time when he may have fought with a sibling, friend, or close relative, but it was his fault. (2) Help the child list things that make him angry with others. (3) Pray with the child to help him learn not to get angry.

NOTES

Noah Builds an Ark

Scripture: Genesis 6:11-22

Memory: Genesis 6:14
Make yourself an ark of cypress wood; make rooms in the ark, and cover it inside and out with pitch.

Memory verse for younger children:
Make yourself an ark of cypress wood.

Meditation: It is hard to imagine the ridicule Noah might have faced as he began to build this ark. First of all, it had never rained before, so the idea of a flood was probably difficult for the people to get their minds around. Secondly, the length of this ark was 300 cubits. Most likely, this was the standard cubit of 18", which means this ark was about as long as one and a half football fields. It was a tremendous undertaking. In this text we are told Noah brought two of every kind of animal. Subsequent texts reveal that there were more of the "clean" animals, although the law had not yet been given which would designate clean from unclean.

We are not given any indication in this text that Noah questioned what God told him to do. There is no evidence that he tried to convert his neighbors, so they could be saved. He was too busy being a carpenter to be an evangelist.

Noah's faith in this undertaking is often underestimated. Why did he believe God and follow these incredible instructions? How did he endure what must have been severe difficulty, frustration and ridicule?

Prayer: Thank you Lord that you helped Noah save all the animals. Thank you that he obeyed you. Amen.

For Discussion: Help the child imagine how the animals might have known to come to Noah. Also talk about how so many animals might have fit on this vessel, even as huge as it is. What would some of the problems have been? Talk about how special it was that God provided care for all these animals.

Activity: (1) Try to find a Noah's Ark set with animals and people. Help the child act out the story. (2)You can create a good counting activity for the youngest children: have them count out two of each animal, and the eight people. (3) Let the child tell the story to you. (4) Help the child name the ways in which God takes care of her.

NOTES

Noah and His Family are Saved

Scripture: Genesis 7:1-5; 8:1

Memory: Genesis 7:4
For in seven days I will send rain on the earth for forty days and forty nights.

Memory verse for younger children:
I will send rain on the earth for forty days and forty nights.

Meditation: Think about the longest time you have ever had to put your life aside because of weather. Imagine doing this for 40 days and nights. No relief, nowhere to go, and a boat load of animals. As indicated previously, it had never rained before. Not only did water come from the sky, but from the wells of the earth. All living creatures were destroyed, except the life that rode on that ark, and perhaps marine life. Noah, his family and the animals were in the ark for one year and ten days. They had to wait for the water to go down and the ground to dry. No wonder they offered sacrifices to God.

As God did when he created life, God told them to be fruitful and multiply. Three young men and their wives did a very good job of this. There was something new after the flood: people were allowed to eat meat. Maybe they had to get rid of some of the animals that were produced during the year.

Prayer: Dear God, thank you for bringing new life into the world. Thank you that you didn't destroy everything. Amen.

 For Discussion: How did all the animals know where to go when they left the ark? How did some get in the arctic and Antarctic, and some stayed right where they were? How did Noah feed all the animals on the ark?

Activity: (1) Draw pictures of the animals leaving the ark. (2) Help the child think about how many more animals might have been born on the ark. (3) Find some stories about modern day sightings of the Ark in Turkey.

NOTES

The Creator Makes a Promise

Scripture: Genesis 9:12-17

Memory: Genesis 9:13
I have set my bow in the clouds, and it shall be a sign of the covenant between me and the earth.

Memory verse for younger children:
I have set my bow in the clouds.

 **Meditation:** God made a promise to Noah: never again would he destroy the earth with water. We can be reminded of that promise every time we see a rainbow. This covenant was made not only between the Creator and humanity, but also the Creator and the earth. Again, we see God treating a rainbow, seemingly inanimate, as if it was living and comprehending. This covenant is everlasting, and there has never been a hint of it being revoked.

The rainbow is not only a reminder to us; God says that it will be a reminder to the Divine as well as to all life on earth. That is an interesting concept: God created a reminder for God.

 Prayer: Lord, rainbows are so pretty. Thank you that every time I see one, I can remember that you made a promise. Amen.

 For Discussion: What conditions must be present for a rainbow to be seen? Can we touch a rainbow? Can we follow a rainbow and find its beginning/end? What do some stories tell us is at the end of a rainbow?

Activity: (1) Read some stories that have rainbows in them. What are some common factors? (2) Using a prism or oil on water, show the child how we can duplicate a rainbow. (3) When you see a rainbow, help the child distinguish the pattern of color.

NOTES

3

The Lord Starts a New Family

The Lord Calls Abram

Scripture: Genesis 12:1-5

Memory: Genesis 12:1
Now the LORD said to Abram, "Go from your country and your kindred and your father's house to the land that I will show you."

Memory verse for younger children:
Now the LORD said to Abram, "Go from your country."

Meditation: Abram and his family had already moved from their native home of Ur. Now the Lord calls them to go even further. Abram's response to the Divine is interesting, because he was firmly embedded in a culture of idols, gods which did not give guidance to people. They were credited with bringing fertility or famine, but not for giving personal direction. That Abram would respond to this God who spoke shows great insight from him and the family that followed him.

Moving is never easy, especially when we are going far away from the familiarity of family and friends to an unfamiliar place. Help the child understand that Abram did not go alone. He went with God's promise that he would be blessed and that future generations would honor him.

Prayer: Thank you Lord for helping Abram when he moved and for helping me. Amen.

For Discussion: If the child is familiar with moving, help him express how he felt when he moved. If he has never moved, help him imagine what it might be like. Tell him that Abram moved to a land where he did not know anyone. How would the child feel about that? Remind the child that God made a promise to Abram and he would always be with him. Discuss what difference that might make to the child.

Activity: (1) Look at a map and find a location distant from your residence. Plan an imaginary move to that place. How will it be different? What will you take? Whom will you see? What will be most difficult to leave? (2)Talk with the child about members of your family who no longer live near you. Did the child know them? If not, help the child learn about people who were part of his family before he was born.

NOTES

Abraham and Sarah Have a Baby

Scripture: Genesis 21:1-7

Memory: Genesis 21: 2
Sarah conceived and bore Abraham a son in his old age, at the time of which God had spoken to him.

Memory verse for younger children:
Sarah bore Abraham a son.

 **Meditation:** The promise Abraham took to Canaan with him is now on the way to fulfillment: Sarah is about to give birth to Isaac, the child of promise. Isaac will be the grandfather of the twelve men for whom all the tribes of Israel will be named. Even though Abraham and Sarah are very old, the Lord did a wonderful thing by keeping the promise and giving them a son.

Your child might be curious about changes in some of the names as we go along: Abram to Abraham (father of many); Sarai to Sarah; and, for the grandson, Jacob to Israel. Help the child understand that for ancient people, names had great meanings. They actually told something about the person. When Sarah found out she would have a child, she laughed. The name of that child, the child whose birth is portrayed in this passage, is Isaac, which means "he will laugh" or "laughter."

 Prayer: Lord, it is good that you still do miracles. Help me see the miracles you do in my life. Amen.

For Discussion: Talk with the child about how her name was chosen. If the child knows people eighty years or older, talk about how difficult it would be for them to have a child. Explain to the child that the birth of Isaac was a wonderful miracle that God did, and to experience childbirth at that age is very unusual.

Activity: (1) Through some research or a "name" book, help the child understand the meaning of her name. (2) If there is a baby in the family or at a friend's house, help the child talk with the baby's parents about what they have to do to take care of the baby. (3) Talk about miracles, and events the child might consider a miracle.

NOTES

God Tests Abraham (Part 1)

Scripture: Overall: Genesis 22:2-18. This Part: Genesis 22:2-9

Memory: Genesis 22:2
He said, "Take your son, your only son Isaac, whom you love, and go to the land of Moriah, and offer him there as a burnt offering on one of the mountains that I shall show you."

Memory verse for younger children:
"Take your son and offer him."

Meditation: In some Jewish literature, Abraham protests that he has two sons (Ishmael) although he loves both of them. However, Ishmael was not the child of promise. Isaac was. How incongruous does it seem that God would tell Abraham to sacrifice this precious son? Although it may not have been widespread, there was a practice of child sacrifice in Abraham's time, so offering his son to fire was not a totally new idea. Where is the promise in sacrifice? As we examine the text preceding this event, we find that Isaac would have been a young man, not a little boy. He questions his father's actions, but he neither protests nor resists.

Because of his willingness to make this sacrifice, Abraham is called the father of faith. Did he believe the Almighty would immediately restore his son? What understanding did he have of an afterlife? We don't know Abraham's thoughts, and he voices no protest. Help your child understand that this was a very unusual event, and the boy does not die, as we will see.

 Prayer: It is scary to think of a daddy hurting his son. Help me not be afraid. Amen.

For Discussion: Talk with the child about difficulties you would have in following the command that Abraham followed. Be sure that the child knows that burning children in fire was something that the Lord hated (Jeremiah 19:5; 32:35). God loves us and would never want to hurt us, or have our parents hurt us.

Activity: (1) Help the child put herself in Isaac's place as he and Abraham go on this journey. Is she afraid? Is the wood heavy? What is she thinking? (2) Ask the child to explain her understanding of "God will provide a lamb." Have the child draw a lamb. Read a book about sheep. Tell the child that Jesus is called the Lamb of God.

NOTES

God Tests Abraham (Part 2)

Scripture: Overall: Genesis 22:2-18. This Part: Genesis 22:10-18

Memory: Genesis 22:12
He (angel of the Lord) said, "Do not lay your hand on the boy or do anything to him; for now I know that you fear God, since you have not withheld your son, your only son, from me."

Memory verse for younger children:
"Do not lay your hand on the boy."

 **Meditation:** No doubt, Abraham would have struck the blow if the Lord had not stopped him, through the angel. Angels are messengers, but sometimes it is hard to distinguish between the Lord's presence and an angel's presence. In whatever way the presence was described, it was the message of the Lord. Abraham had passed the test! The child of promise was saved! However, there seems to be some consequences of this event. In verse 19, we see that Abraham returns home. Where is Isaac? Also, we are very shortly told of the death of Sarah. Did she hear what had happened on that mountain? Is it possible that there is some dissonance now between father and son? We don't hear of them together again, even though Abraham ensures Isaac has a wife. When Abraham dies, both Isaac and Ishmael bury him. Rejoice with the child that Isaac has been saved and Abraham showed how faithful he was to the Lord.

 Prayer: Thank you Lord that Abraham did not have to kill Isaac.

Help me show you how much I love you. Amen.

 For Discussion: Help the child imagine the feelings of Isaac when Abraham sacrifices the ram. Discuss the possibilities of happiness, anger, fear and sadness. Even though this was a test of how much Abraham loved God, does the child think that what happened to Isaac was fair?

Activity: Try to act out this scenario, from departure through the sacrifice of the ram. Let the child be Isaac, Abraham and the angel of the Lord.

NOTES

Isaac Takes a Wife

Scripture: Genesis 24:10-15, 67

Memory: Genesis 24:67

Then Isaac brought her into his mother Sarah's tent. He took Rebekah, and she became his wife; and he loved her. So Isaac was comforted after his mother's death.

Memory verse for younger children:
Rebekah became his wife.

Meditation: This is actually the story of a faithful servant. He prays to the Lord, in the name of his master, that the Lord would give him a sign, and direct him to the right person. As the prayer ends, there is Rebekah. Rebekah is a relative of Abraham and Sarah, but that was more acceptable at that time. Abraham had given his servant strict instructions that a wife was not to be taken from the land in which they lived, a land filled with people who did not follow the Lord. The servant was to go back to Abraham's family for a bride, but was not to take Isaac back there. The child of promise was to stay in the land of promise.

The servant of Abraham tells Rebekah's family all that had happened to bring him to their tent. How could they refuse his request that Rebekah return with him to be the wife of Abraham's son? They asked Rebekah if she wanted to go immediately, without all the preparation for a wedding, and she agrees. When she gets to Isaac, he loves her, and they are married.

Help the child understand that marriages were arranged by parents and the servant was helping fulfill this arrangement.

 Prayer: The servant was faithful to Abraham, his master. Help me be faithful to my parents. Amen.

 For Discussion: Talk with the child about any expectations of marriage they may have (listen for reflections of your own marriage). Ask the child if they would want to marry someone they did not know. Talk about mail-order marriages you might be familiar with. Talk about ways the child may have seen the Lord answer prayers.

 Activity: Plan an imaginary wedding with the child. If they have ever been in or attended a wedding, help them remember some of the things that happened.

NOTES

_____

_____

_____

_____

_____

_____

_____

_____

_____

_____

_____

_____

_____

_____

Rebekah Gives Birth to Twins

Scripture: Genesis 25:21-26

Memory: Genesis 25:21
Isaac prayed to the LORD for his wife, because she was barren; and the LORD granted his prayer, and his wife Rebekah conceived.

Memory verse for younger children:
Isaac prayed and the LORD granted his prayer.

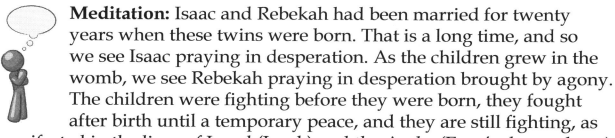

Meditation: Isaac and Rebekah had been married for twenty years when these twins were born. That is a long time, and so we see Isaac praying in desperation. As the children grew in the womb, we see Rebekah praying in desperation brought by agony. The children were fighting before they were born, they fought after birth until a temporary peace, and they are still fighting, as manifested in the lives of Israel (Jacob) and the Arabs (Esau's descendants). The Almighty tells Rebekah that two nations are in her womb, and yet, as the birth is described, the fact of twins is presented as new information. I am sure it was no surprise to Rebekah.

As these boys grow, the love that we saw between Isaac and Rebekah at the outset is severely challenged. They each have a favorite child, and this causes major problems within the family. Because of his mother's deceitfulness, the youngest, Jacob, is forced to leave, and returns to his mother's family. He is there long enough to marry two sisters and their maids, and father at least thirteen children. The twelve males in this family become the tribes of Israel, the name which the Almighty later bestows on Jacob. Jacob and his family return to his home, at which time a tenuous peace is established with his brother Esau. We see little more of the interaction between these two twins.

Prayer: Thank you Lord for opportunities to make peace with people who may not like us. Amen.

For Discussion: Talk with the child about some twins you may both know. How are they different? How are they alike?

Activity: (1) Recall your last visit to grandparents. Discuss with the child the things he likes—and may not like—about visiting grandparents. (2) Help the child imagine what it would be like to be so afraid of a sibling that he had to leave home to be safe. What feelings would the child experience? (3) If you know someone with twin babies, ask them to share with the child some of the special joys and concerns with twins.

NOTES

4

Abraham's Family Goes to Egypt

Joseph's Brothers Sell Him (Part 1)

Scripture: Genesis 37:12-36. This Part: Genesis 37:12-28

Memory: Genesis 37:28
When some Midianite traders passed by, they drew Joseph up, lifting him out of the pit, and sold him to the Ishmaelites for twenty pieces of silver. And they took Joseph to Egypt.

Memory verse for younger children:
They took Joseph to Egypt.

Meditation: Joseph was the favorite son of his father, even though he had a younger brother Benjamin, probably an infant. His older half-brothers resented their father's favoritism. Joseph also had dreams of his family bowing down to him, which fueled the anger of his brothers. Their first thought was to kill him. His brothers Reuben and Judah, the forefather of the line of Jesus, recommended saving the boy's life, and so he was sold. Joseph is believed to be a teenager at this point, so you might imagine his despair as he is sold to the caravan going to Egypt.

Whether he had been arrogant or just immature in his boasts, his boasting was over. The older brothers were very unkind, and as we will see later, dishonest. Your child probably knows that there are mean people in the world. The meanness seems more exaggerated since these are all family members.

Prayer: Lord, help me never be mean to anyone, especially members of my family. Amen.

For Discussion: Discuss with the child some of the things Joseph went through: thrown into a pit with no water, then pulled up and given to complete strangers, who took him far away from his family. How would the child respond? Would the child be angry with his brothers?

Activity: (1) Help the child write a letter to the brothers as if he was Joseph. Tell the brothers how he feels. (2) Describe some of the things that might have happened on the way to Egypt (imagination).

NOTES

Joseph's Brothers Sell Him (Part 2)

Scripture: Genesis 37:12-36. This Part: Genesis 37:13-36

Memory: Genesis 37:36
Meanwhile the Midianites had sold him in Egypt to Potiphar, one of
Pharaoh's officials, the captain of the guard.

Memory verse for younger children:
Midianites had sold him in Egypt to Potiphar.

Meditation: What a downfall Joseph has experienced. From a
favored son of a wealthy herder to being a slave to a soldier in
Egypt. For now, however, we are left to share the sorrow of his
father, as his sons lead him to believe that Joseph is dead. Dipping
the beloved coat in blood was a harsh deceit. His beloved wife
Rachel, the mother of Joseph and Benjamin, is gone, and now
Rachel's oldest son is gone. Jacob had been deceitful toward his brother
Esau, and now he is being repaid. What goes around truly does come back
around. We are told that Jacob's children try to comfort him. Do you think
it would have been any comfort if the boys had confessed and admitted
what they had really done? Help the child understand the sorrow of Jacob,
caused by the unkindness and deceit of his sons.

Prayer: Lord, it is very sad when someone dies. Thank you that
you comfort us. Amen.

For Discussion: Explain to the child that being a slave to someone means you have no rights and someone controls everything you do. Also, talk about a death the child knew about. If the child was close to the deceased, help her recall how she felt.

Activity: Acting out something always gives us better understanding. There are several roles here: the brothers who wanted to kill Joseph, the brother who found Joseph gone, the father and, of course, Joseph. Let the child portray their impression of each of these.

NOTES

Joseph in Egypt

Scripture: Genesis 41: 1-7; 9-14; 28-32; 39-41; 46-49; 53-57

Memory: Genesis 41:39
So Pharaoh said to Joseph, "Since God has shown you all this, there is no one so discerning and wise as you."

Memory verse for younger children:
God has shown you all this.

 **Meditation:** God really blessed Joseph in Egypt. His master's wife tried to seduce him. Joseph refused to comply because he believed God would not want him to commit such an act, so she had him tossed into jail. There he met two servants of Pharaoh whose dreams he interpreted. Both dreams came true: one servant was put to death, the other was returned to the service of Pharaoh. When Pharaoh begins to have his disturbing dreams, it is this servant who tells Pharaoh about Joseph, the dream interpreter, still in jail. Pharaoh recognizes the power of a god upon Joseph's life—Egyptians had many gods—and gives him the authority to prepare for the years when food would not be plentiful. Joseph, after about thirteen years, goes from slave to ruler. Help the child understand that only God could work such a wonderful thing.

 Prayer: Dear Lord, thank you for guiding and protecting Joseph and for guiding and protecting me. Amen.

For Discussion: Talk about Pharaoh's weird dreams: sickly cattle eating healthy cattle; bad corn eating good corn. How did Joseph have the power to tell Pharaoh what these dreams meant? Be sure the child knows that it was God that helped Joseph do all these things. What are some of the dreams you have had?

Activity: Help the child interpret the dreams with drawings. Have the child draw a picture of Joseph as ruler in Egypt.

NOTES

Joseph's Family Comes to Egypt

Scripture: Genesis 42-46, various selections: 42:1-10; 17-26; 35-38. 43:1-5; 11-14; 26-30. 45:1-7; 25-28

Memory: Genesis 45:5
And now do not be distressed, or angry with yourselves, because you sold me here; for God sent me before you to preserve life.

Memory verse for younger children:
God sent me before you.

Meditation: This is a huge passage that could be divided up into several sessions. Joseph's brothers came to Egypt to buy grain, because the famine has spread throughout the land. Joseph is the ruler selling the grain, and so they bow before him, thus fulfilling the dreams Joseph had as a teenager. Joseph toys with his brothers for a while, not disclosing who he is. He has his cup put into one of their bags, then had them brought back as thieves; he demanded that the youngest son Benjamin be brought and gave Benjamin extra portions of food and clothing, adding to their frustration and confusion. Even though Joseph forgives them, he gets a little bit of revenge in their discomfort. They do recognize that they might be receiving the wages of their sin against their brother, but they don't realize that it is the brother paying the wages. Help the child see how God worked through all these events to bring this family back together.

Prayer: Dear God, help me always forgive those who are mean to me. Amen.

 For Discussion: Help the child imagine how Joseph felt when he saw his brothers. How did the brothers feel when they found out the ruler who sold the grain to them was their brother? How did Jacob feel when he heard that Joseph was alive?

Activity: (1) Help the child make a list of people he might want to forgive for doing bad things to him. Whom might the child need to forgive him? (2) Let the child act out how Jacob (Israel) might have acted when he learned that Joseph was alive.

NOTES

5

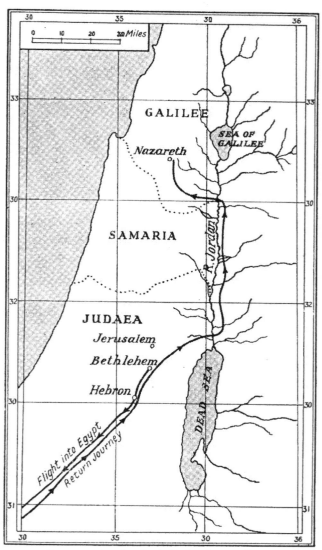

Journey taken by the holy family into Egypt
and back in their home in Nazareth

Abraham's Family Leaves Egypt

Moses is Born and Adopted

Scripture: Exodus 2:1-10

Memory: Exodus 2:10
When the child grew up, she brought him to Pharaoh's daughter, and she took him as her son. She named him Moses, "because," she said, "I drew him out of the water."

Memory verse for younger children:
She named him Moses.

**Meditation:** Some background for this passage: The Hebrews who came to Egypt through Joseph had multiplied greatly. Joseph and all his generation are gone, and a new Pharaoh who does not know Joseph sits on the throne. The Hebrews are seen as a threat, and so they are enslaved. When this does not reduce the numbers, a command is put out to slaughter all the male Hebrew children. The descendants of Abraham are saved from this process by sympathetic midwives. The attempt to save this child from the decree led to these events. How merciful of The Holy One to see that the child is nursed and raised by his mother. The Lord provided for a wonderful upbringing for this child, because he was very precious in the Lord's sight, as all children are.

The term "Hebrew" is not generally used to describe the Israelites by other Israelites. It is a term used by outsiders and enemies of Israel. Today, those same Israelites are known as Jews.

Prayer: Dear Lord, thank you that even little children are precious in your sight. Amen.

For Discussion: Talk about the basket/boat that the baby's mother made for him. Discuss some things that might have happened to the child set sail on the Nile, a tropical river. Ask the child how he might feel about being set out on a river in a basket. Talk about the way the Lord arranged circumstances so the child could be raised by his mother. Talk about adoption.

Activity: (1) Try to help the child make a little basket, using raffia or dried grasses. (2) Help the child draw a picture of the River and the child in a basket. (3) Use a picture book to help the child learn about Egypt.

NOTES

"I Am" Talks to Moses

Scripture: Exodus 3:1-10

Memory: Exodus 3:4
When the LORD saw that he had turned aside to see, God called to him out of the bush, "Moses, Moses!" And he said, "Here I am."

Memory verse for younger children:
He said, "Here I am."

Meditation: As Moses grew up, he seemed to have some understanding of his background. When he killed an Egyptian in an attempt to protect one of the Hebrews, he had to flee Egypt. He went into the wilderness, married and became a sheep herder. It is in this context that "I Am" appears to Moses. The story of the fiery bush that is not consumed is well known. At his mother's knee, Moses had certainly heard of the God of his ancestors. Now he has encountered this God, who describes the increasing hardship of Moses' people in Egypt. Moses stands in the holy presence and receives a commission to return to Egypt and set God's people free. God may not appear in the form of a flaming bush these days, but he still gets his message across to those with ears and hearts to hear.

Prayer: Holy God of Moses, thank you for talking to me as you talked to Moses. Amen.

For Discussion: Help the child imagine how a bush might burn without being damaged by the flame. Tell the child that prayer is the way we talk to God, and that God talks to us in a number of ways: through situations, other people, and the Bible, to name a few. Get a book about sheep and share information with the child.

Activity: (1) Under very controlled conditions, try to find some things that might not be affected by fire. (2) Help the child write a brief prayer. (3) If there are any sheepherders in your area, try to go and talk to them about raising sheep.

NOTES

Moses Returns to Egypt (Part 1)

Scripture: Exodus 5:1-21 This Part: Genesis 5:1-9

Memory: Exodus 5:1
Afterward Moses and Aaron went to Pharaoh and said, "Thus says the LORD, the God of Israel, 'Let my people go, so that they may celebrate a festival to me in the wilderness.'"

Memory verse for younger children:
"Let my people go."

Meditation: Many believe that the Hebrews made the pyramids. While they may have made similar structures, the main pyramids were built in an era different from the time we believe the people were enslaved in Egypt. There was always some kind of major construction going on, e.g., tombs, monuments and mortuaries, and slave labor was cheap. Certainly Pharaoh and his rulers would not want to lose this source of help.

Egyptians worshiped many different gods, so the god of the Hebrews would not have made much of an impression on them. The Egyptians were skilled in magic arts, highly educated and cosmopolitan, so a sheepherder would have had a difficult time getting their attention. We are using the term "Hebrews" in these thoughts because that is what the Egyptians would have called the people, but actually an Israelite would not have called another Israelite a Hebrew unless they wanted to offend.

Prayer: Dear Lord, thank you that you cared for the Israelites and you care for me. Amen.

For Discussion: Talk about what being a construction worker under slavery might mean (it would be different from the slavery Joseph knew). Help the child understand how Moses was not important for the Egyptians, so they would not have wanted to listen to him. Talk about how important these people were to God, and how God wanted to set them free from the very difficult conditions in which they lived.

Activity: (1) Look at pictures of pyramids and help the child understand the complexity of these tombs. (2) Read an article about brick making. Help the child use mud and dry grass to make a brick, baking it in the sun. Talk about how many it might take to make even a small pyramid.

NOTES

Moses Returns to Egypt (Part 2)

Scripture: Exodus 5:1-21; This Part: Genesis 5:10-21

Memory: Exodus 5:21
They said to them, "The LORD look upon you and judge! You have brought us into bad odor with Pharaoh and his officials, and have put a sword in their hand to kill us."

Memory verse for younger children:
"You have put a sword in their hand."

Meditation: Not only do Pharaoh and his rulers ridicule Moses, but, because of his demands, they have made the work harder for the people Moses is trying to help, and the Israelites have turned on Moses. Many of these people probably do not even know about the God of Abraham, Isaac and Jacob, their ancient ancestors. Why should they believe Moses? Their labor was hard enough when they were given all they needed to do their work. Now, having to gather their own straw, but make the same amount of bricks, it is no wonder they want nothing to do with Moses.

Many of the responses to Moses' demands made life not only harder for the people, but also for Moses. I am sure there were times he wanted to give up. It would have taken a very faithful heart to continue to listen to God and put up with continued rejection.

Prayer: Precious Lord, thank you that you always listen to me, even if others do not. Amen.

For Discussion: Talk about the reasons the people may not have wanted to listen to or believe Moses. Talk about times the child may have felt no one wanted to listen to her. Encourage the child to believe that God will always listen to her. Talk about what the Scripture's use of "bad odor" might mean (literally, "you make us stink before them," or "they hate us").

 Activity: Learning more about Egypt and the gods they worshiped will be helpful for the next session involving the plagues, all of which relate to one of the Egyptian gods.

NOTES

Ten Plagues Bring Freedom

Scripture: Exodus Chapters 7-13: 7:1-5, 20-21; 8:8-15,17-19, 24-28; 9:6-7, 10-15, 18-26; 10:12-15, 19-20, 27-29; 11:1-3; 12:25-32. You might prefer to read this section in a children's Bible or Bible story book.

Memory: Exodus 7:2
You shall speak all that I command you, and your brother Aaron shall tell Pharaoh to let the Israelites go out of his land.

Memory verse for younger children:
Tell Pharaoh to let the Israelites go.

Meditation: Water turned to blood. Frogs. Gnats. Flies. Pestilence. Boils. Hail. Locusts. The death of the firstborn. What an incredible litany of suffering God brought upon the Egyptians because their leader would not relinquish his pride and let the children of Israel leave the land. Studying these plagues closely, we can see some progression: frogs would want to escape bloody waters; dead frogs would collect flies; dead animals would bring pestilence and disease. The final blow, the death of the firstborn of all households where blood was not put on the door frame, gives us an idea of the Pharaoh of the period. It would not have been Ramses, who would have died, because he was firstborn. The Passover was instituted during this liberation. The covering of the blood on the door lintels is the picture of the blood of Christ that covers our sin, so that death might pass over us. Help the child understand that nothing is too great for a God who loves and leads.

Prayer: God of Moses, thank you that you can do all things for your people. Amen.

 For Discussion: The plagues, Pharaoh's response to the plagues, and God's work in Pharaoh's heart should prompt much discussion. Why would God want to harden Pharaoh's heart so he would not let the people go?

Activity: As you discuss each of the plagues, have the child draw his impression of what is going on.

NOTES

Israelites in the Wilderness

Crossing the Sea

Scripture: Exodus 14:19-31

Memory: Exodus 14:22
The Israelites went into the sea on dry ground, the waters forming a wall for them on their right and on their left.

Memory verse for younger children:
The Israelites went into the sea on dry ground.

 **Meditation:** While some translations talk about the "army" of Israel, a better translation of the Hebrew word is "camp." For the time being, this relieves us of part of the military connotation, although we certainly see that again. Both the angel of the Lord and the pillar that led and followed the people represent the presence of the Lord. These actively delay the Egyptians until Israel can cross on the dry ground. As the Egyptians enter the river bed, the waters begin to crash down upon them. For a brief while at least, this miracle achieves the desired effect: Israel fears and believes in the Lord and in Moses his servant. God goes to wondrous extremes to enable his children to fear and believe.

 Prayer: Lord, thank you for saving your people from those who want to hurt them. Amen.

For Discussion: Help the child imagine how the waters divided, stood up and allowed the Israelites to pass, then came down upon the Egyptians. Talk about what the people must have been feeling about all that had happened: fear, amazement, surprise, sadness (leaving a place they had been all their lives), relief, and wonder.

 Activity: Obtain the movie "Ten Commandments" and at least look at this part of the movie. The visual effects are pretty awesome.

NOTES

Bread and Meat

Scripture: Exodus 16:11-16

Memory: Exodus 16:15
When the Israelites saw it, they said to one another, "What is it?" For they did not know what it was. Moses said to them, "It is the bread that the LORD has given you to eat."

Memory verse for younger children:
"It is the bread that the LORD has given you to eat."

Meditation: The interpretation of the question "what is it," in the Hebrew, is *manhu*, thus the name for this bread: manna. They ate this bread for forty years, until they moved into the land and produced their own food. This bread not only nourished the Israelites, but it was an ongoing test. Five days a week they were to gather only what they needed. Any extra spoiled. On the day before the Sabbath, they gathered two days worth, and none spoiled. Also, none was available on the Sabbath. The people often tested (and frustrated) the faithful Provider by trying to collect extra and by going out on the Sabbath. They did not want to follow the Lord's leading, despite the miracles they had already witnessed. Their Provider was providing them with food and boundaries.

Prayer: Thank you, Great Provider, that you always see to the needs of your people, even when it is sometimes hard for us. Amen.

For Discussion: Talk with the child about eating the same food every day all of his life. Our Scripture also talks about the time that meat is provided. Talk about having so many birds around you that you just have to reach out to get dinner. Also, the people ate so much meat that they got sick. Talk with the child about this possibility.

Activity: (1) Look at a food pyramid and help the child identify his favorite of all the food groups. Talk about the different nutrition obtained from these. (2) Help the child list all the nutrients that the manna might have provided and how each of these might have helped the people (e.g., carbohydrates (bread) gave them energy to walk long distances).

NOTES

Ten Important Rules (Part 1)

Scripture: Exodus 20:1-17; This part: Exodus 20:1-11

Memory: Exodus 20:3
"You shall have no other gods before me."

Meditation: These rules, which we have come to call the Ten Commandments, are divided into two parts: those which relate to humanity and the Deity, and those which relate to interactions among humanity. Although given thousands of years ago, these rules are just as relevant to us today as they were to the people then, especially those describing person to person relationships. In this reading we will focus on the rules which describe what the Deity expects from those bearing the Name. God knows that people can't be all they should be if they do not have boundaries, rules which guide their walk in life. Like any good parent, God knows that rules help us live better lives.

Prayer: Dear Lord, sometimes rules are hard, but I know we have rules in our lives to help us know how to be good. Amen.

For Discussion: Talk about why we should only worship one God. Why would the Deity not want people to make images (pictures, carvings) of animals or other things on earth? (They might become idols more important than God). Remember previous discussions about the day of rest. Talk about how it was now a rule that God expected the people to follow. Help the child understand some different way the Lord's name might be misused (e.g., saying "O my God" all the time, without meaning).

Activity: (1) Look at different pictures of Jesus or God. Talk about how these might break the commandments. (2) If your church has stained glass windows, look at them with the child and talk about how these might relate to the commandments. Ask the child if he thinks it is okay to have these pictures and why (one possibility: danger of turning them into idols).

NOTES

Ten Important Rules (Part 2)

Scripture: Exodus 20:1-17; This part: Exodus 20:12-17

Memory: Exodus 20:12
Honor your father and your mother, so that your days may be long in the land that the LORD your God is giving you.

Memory verse for younger children:
Honor your father and your mother.

Meditation: The most important part of this section for the child will be the first admonition about honoring parents. Actually, I think this is more for adult children, but it doesn't hurt to start training early. Other rules the child may need to hear about are: not bearing false witness (lying); not stealing and not coveting (being jealous and wanting something so much that you might be willing to take it). For younger children, adultery and murder will not be an issue. You just might help the child understand that the Lord wants us to try to do the right things all the time. We might sometimes act like we don't know what the right thing is, but if we look really deep inside ourselves, we will know. Conscience and conviction by the Lord should always work together in our lives. Help the child understand that treating other people right is part of loving God.

Prayer: Thank you Lord, for showing me how to treat other people in good ways. Amen.

For Discussion: What does "honor your parents" mean to the child? How has the child done this? How will the child do this in the future? Has the child ever taken things that didn't belong to him? What was—or can be—done about this? Has the child ever lied about anything? Talk about how one lie can often lead to many lies.

Activity: (1) Again, the movie "Ten Commandments" could be helpful in helping the child visualize this passage. (2) Also, help the child list ways she will follow these last six (four) commandments.

NOTES

A Golden Idol

Scripture: Exodus 32:1-6

Memory: Exodus 32:4
He took the gold from them, formed it in a mold, and cast an *image of a calf*; and they said, "*These are your gods*, O Israel, who brought you up out of the land of Egypt!"

Memory verse for younger children:
Aaron said, "A Golden calf is your God."

Meditation: The irony of this event is almost humorous. As Moses is being given the laws, Aaron, his brother and assistant, is abetting the people in breaking almost all of them. It wasn't humorous to either God or Moses, however. It cost these people dearly. The saddest thing about this is how this hastily-made golden figure replaced the Creator who truly did bring the people out of slavery and oppression in Egypt. What kind of fools were these people? We can put ourselves in their place. How many times each day do we experience some good thing, and then give the credit to someone or something other than the Lord who was actually the provider? Awareness of this should help us determine to work harder at recognizing the Lord's hand at work in our lives.

Prayer: I want to see you at work in my life, Lord. Help me always see you. Amen.

For Discussion: Talk about why it is important to recognize that God is still at work in our lives. We credit many things when we should credit God. Talk about how we turn some of our possessions into idols (e.g., TV, video games, toys) by thinking more about them than we do God.

Activity: You might not want to use the movie "Ten Commandments" for this section, because of the behavior of the people. (1) Visit a museum and show the child some idols from ancient cultures. Talk about the different variety: people and animals made of many different substances. Ask the child why he thinks people worshiped these different idols.

NOTES

A Place to Worship

Scripture: Exodus 40:1-11

Memory: Exodus 40: 2
On the first day of the first month you shall set up the tabernacle of the tent of meeting.

Memory verse for younger children:
Set up the tabernacle of the tent of meeting.

Meditation: The One Worthy of Worship goes into great detail describing this tent of worship. There are specific reasons for the decoration, the placement and the use of each item and the structure itself. Why? In John 1:14, where we are told that the Word became flesh and dwelt among us. The word for *dwelt* and the word for *tabernacle* used here are related in the Greek. Jesus *tabernacled* among us. The tabernacle in the wilderness and all of its fixtures are a picture of Christ. Many of the furnishings are pictures of things which other Scriptures tell us are actually in the heavenly places. The altar in the earthly tabernacle is a picture of the true altar upon which the precious blood of Jesus was poured out following his sacrifice. That is why Christians no longer make sacrifices of flesh: Jesus is our sacrifice. That background aside, the important and relevant thing for the child here is that no matter where we are, God wants to meet with us and tabernacle with us.

Prayer: Thank you, Lord, that you will meet with me no matter where I am or what I am doing. Amen.

For Discussion: Read through this chapter and descriptions of some of the furnishings of the tabernacle. Talk about this tent and how the things in it are different from your place of worship, and how they might be alike. Help the child understand that everything in this tabernacle had special meanings and purposes, because they represented eternal things (e.g., the bread on the table is a picture of Jesus, the Bread of Life). Help the child understand the difference between temporal and eternal.

Activity: (1) If you can find an example or a picture of a model of the tabernacle, go over that with the child. (2) Go to different places and help the child understand how they might meet with God in those places. (3) Explore different ways of talking to God: thanking God for beautiful trees and flowers in a park; praising the power of God as you look at a waterfall; thanking God for the beautiful songs of birds.

NOTES

The Promised Land

A New Leader

Scripture: Joshua 1:1-9

Memory: Joshua 1:5
No one shall be able to stand against you all the days of your life. As I was with Moses, so I will be with you; I will not fail you or forsake you.

Memory verse for younger children:
I will be with you.

 **Meditation:** Joshua had been groomed for leadership for many years. He went with spies into the new land. He came back and, with Caleb, gave an optimistically positive report of the possibilities. Ten other spies came back and discouraged the people (Numbers 13:21-14:10). Leadership is Joshua's reward for trusting God rather than his own eyes and senses. While Moses led God's army, but engaged in little military action, Joshua is truly a military leader. Joshua is one of the few people in Scripture in whom we see no weakness or rebellion. He is faithful to the Lord in all his days. He truly knew that God was with him, and he lived his life based on that knowledge.

 Prayer: Thank you Lord that when I feel all alone, you are with me. Amen.

 For Discussion: Talk about responsibility, helping the child understand some of the responsibilities of his life. Talk about the nearness of God: how he knows what we think; he knows our "hearts" (help the child understand that "heart" is another word for our mind — it is what we are inside, but not physically). Discuss all the benefits of having God always close to us (e.g., we don't have to be afraid; we're never really alone; we can talk to God; God knows what we are going through).

Activity: (1) Since Joshua was a military leader, look in books or a museum for the weapons and battle apparel of the period. Talk about how these are different from military supplies today. (2) If you are not into the military, help the child list different ways that God's presence might be manifest in their lives (e.g., he eats breakfast with me, he watches over me when I sleep).

NOTES

_____

_____

_____

_____

_____

_____

_____

_____

_____

_____

_____

_____

_____

_____

_____

_____

_____

_____

A Special Reminder

Scripture: Joshua 4:1-9

Memory: Joshua 4:7
". . . then you shall tell them that the waters of the Jordan were cut off in front of the ark of the covenant of the LORD. When it crossed over the Jordan, the waters of the Jordan were cut off. So these stones shall be to the Israelites a memorial forever."

Memory verse for younger children:
"These stones shall be to the Israelites a memorial forever."

Meditation: In Scripture, we see several ways that the Eternal One guides people to remember what he has done for them. These twelve stones are one of my favorite examples: this pile of stones was left as a memorial of entry into the Promised Land through divided waters and many other tribulations. This raises a few questions: how many times did the people return to see the stones? How long were the stones there? How big were the stones? (They were carried on the shoulders). Did anyone ever really ask "What do these stones mean?" I think all those things might take a second seat to the fact that Joshua, under God's leading, led the people to establish a reminder, whether or not it was ever used. Memory is very important to Jews, e.g., memory of the Passover, memory of the Holocaust. Whatever any predecessors have gone through, those who are alive today have gone through it also. Memory becomes existence.

Prayer: Loving Lord, help me always to remember the things you do in my life. Amen.

For Discussion: Talk with the child about their memories. What kinds of things help you remember? How far back can you remember? Try to discern if the child is really remembering or if they playing off of someone else's memories.

Activity: (1) Help the child identify the things in his life that help him remember. (2) Create a *memory box* or *memory quilt*. (3) Help the child collect something (fuzz, a word, etc.) from the things that help him remember and put these all together in one place. Pictures can also be helpful in this effort.

NOTES

A Different Judge

Scripture: Judges 4:1-10

Memory: Judges 4:3
Then the Israelites cried out to the LORD for help; for he had nine hundred chariots of iron, and had oppressed the Israelites cruelly twenty years.

Memory verse for younger children:
The Israelites cried out to the LORD for help.

 **Meditation:** There is a cycle of activity within the Book of Judges: the people disobey God; God sends an oppressor; the people cry out for help; God sends a deliverer; the deliverer dies; the people disobey God. The cycle is repeated several times. At one of these times, Deborah is used to deliver the people. Many of the "judges" of this writing are not really judges, but military leaders. Deborah actually seems to do some judging along with her military exploits. I believe that when no men will step forth to do the work of the Lord, God appoints women. Deborah tries to delegate authority to Barak, a man, but he is not willing to accept the responsibility without her presence. In the end, it is another woman, Jael, who gains the victory over the Canaanite oppressor Sisera (Judges 4:17-22).

 Prayer: God of all people, help me to remember that you can use anyone to do your work. Amen.

 For Discussion: Talk about women the child may know who are in leadership positions, especially in the church. What do these women do? Do men work for them? How might these women have gotten into these positions? Help the child understand that while men and women are different, they can do almost all of the same jobs.

Activity: Visit a church where a woman is pastor, or make an appointment with a female judge or a female military officer. Help the child determine some questions to ask them about their work. Other possibilities: female construction worker or any woman working in a job where there are mostly men.

NOTES

_____

_____

_____

_____

_____

_____

_____

_____

_____

_____

_____

_____

_____

_____

Gideon Tests God

Scripture: Judges 6:33-40

Memory: Judges 6:36-37

Then Gideon said to God, "In order to see whether you will deliver Israel by my hand, as you have said, I am going to lay a fleece of wool on the threshing floor; if there is dew on the fleece alone, and it is dry on all the ground, then I shall know that you will deliver Israel by my hand, as you have said."

Memory verse for younger children: "I am going to lay a fleece of wool on the threshing floor."

 **Meditation:** How often have you "put a fleece" before God? How often have you said, "If you, O Lord, do this, I will do this, I will know this, I will go there." It is human nature to want "confirmation" of things. We don't like to be left hanging; we want to know for sure. Gideon had very little faith in God. He eventually did what he was called upon to do, but first he had to find some certainty.

The important thing about this for us is that God honored these requests. The God of Hope wants us to know that we have the promise of Presence, and that Presence will help us do whatever we are called to do. The Lord will not leave us as orphans, but wants us to believe and will provide whatever we might need to help us in that belief.

Prayer: Thank you, Lord, that you help me believe that I can do whatever you want me to do. Amen.

For Discussion: Help the child understand that God may put a call on their heart to do something, even as a child. Ask the child if they feel that God has ever told them to do something. Encourage the child to know that they may not hear words, but may just have a "feeling" of something they are supposed to do or not do.

Activity: (1) Through books or an actual item, help the child understand what a fleece (sheepskin) is. (2) Maybe the child would like to put a "fleece" before God: test something the child might think God would have them do. Make it simple and relevant to the child's life. But be careful. The child may become discouraged if the test is not answered.

NOTES

_____
_____
_____
_____
_____
_____
_____
_____
_____
_____
_____
_____
_____
_____

A Foreigner in the Family

Scripture: Ruth 1:3-5, 14, 16-18; 3:10-13; 4:9-10, 16-17

Memory: Ruth 4:17
The women of the neighborhood gave him a name, saying, "A son has been born to Naomi." They named him Obed; *he became the father of* Jesse, the father of *David.*

Memory verse for younger children:
He *became the grandfather of David.*

 **Meditation:** The last part of the verse above could be extended to read "the father of Jesus," because Jesus is a descendant of David, Israel's greatest king. This foreigner, a Moabite woman named Ruth, is in the genealogy of our Lord. There are times in Scripture when the Moabites are enemies of Israel, and Israel is instructed to exclude enemies from the congregation, and yet we see the inclusion of this foreigner in a very special role. Sometimes, God's instructions seem harsh, and we don't understand the reasons. We do understand that God was trying to create a special people who would be God's people. Once this people is created, all who love God are welcome to join. Ruth's story is one of faithfulness and compassion. She clung to her mother-in-law when she could have returned to her family. Naomi's God became Ruth's God, and so she was welcomed into the family.

 Prayer: God of all people, thank you that you welcome everyone into your family. Amen.

For Discussion: Encourage the child to think about families you know who have "foreigners" in them, especially if they are adopted children. Talk about how foreign children might feel coming to a new land, learning all the many things they have to learn. Help the child identify some things newcomers might have to learn about. Remind the child that God loves people from every country, and that there are people in almost every country who love God.

Activity: Try to visit a family which has at least one person who was not born in this country. Help the child ask questions about what their life was like before, and the changes that they have had to make. Especially help the child to focus on possible differences in their faith walk.

NOTES

A Special Little Boy

Scripture: 1 Samuel 1:9-20

Memory: 1 Samuel 1: 20
In due time Hannah conceived and bore a son. She named him Samuel, for she said, "I have asked him of the LORD."

Memory verse for younger children:
"I have asked him of the LORD."

Meditation: Before you gave birth, did you pray for the children the Lord has given to you? If so, you will want to let the child know this. Hannah prayed for and received a son after promising God she would commit him to the Lord's purposes. She kept her promise. As soon as the child was weaned, she took him to Eli, the priest, who raised him in the temple alongside his own sons. How hard it must have been for this mother to part with her son, but God rewarded her for her faithfulness by giving her other sons. Eli's sons were disobedient to God, but Samuel grew in faithfulness and the contrast was noted by the Israelites. Samuel became a priest, the priest who anointed David as King. His own sons continued in the pattern of Eli's sons, and so the dynasty of priesthood was not continued in Samuel's family. Samuel had the heritage of loving, faithful parents, but did not seem to be so himself.

Prayer: Thank you for parents who love their children and pray for them. Amen.

For Discussion: If your child was longed for and prayed for before birth, definitely let her know this. Talk about some of the things loving parents, who see their children as gifts from God, do for their children: e.g., spend time with them, give them boundaries, teach them about Jesus, take them to church, etc. Talk about how difficult it must have been for Hannah to give up her little boy for the Lord. Tell the child that priests of Samuel's time were "messengers" from God who met God for the people. Now, because of Jesus, we can go directly to God without needing a priest.

Activity: (1) Help the child understand different types of priests: an ancient Jewish priest in the temple of Israel; a modern Jewish Rabbi in a synagogue; a Catholic priest today. Use books and actual visits to help the child understand the differences and similarities. (2) Have the leader of your faith group talk about the tasks they perform as a leader.

NOTES

8

Kings for the People

Saul, the First King

Scripture: 1 Samuel 9:15-27

Memory: 1 Samuel 17
When Samuel saw Saul, the LORD told him, "Here is the man of whom I spoke to you. He it is who shall rule over my people."

Memory verse for younger children:
"Saul shall rule over my people."

 **Meditation:** The Lord wanted to be the only ruler of the people of Israel, but the people clamored for a king like the other nations. Finally, Samuel was given guidance to appoint Saul. Saul was tall, handsome and, at times, incredibly stupid and arrogant. The people were told what it would be like to have a king (1 Samuel 8:10-18), and most of these prophecies were fulfilled in King Solomon, for the most part. The picture was not pretty, but the people insisted on having a king. Israel had seen the Lord their God do an incredible number of things for them, most recently the appointment of judges to liberate them from oppressors. It wasn't enough. If the surrounding nations had kings, they should have a king. Saul came from the smallest clan, Benjamin, and apparently his family was not significant. He was originally rejected by many, yet he was chosen by God as Israel's first king.

 Prayer: Lord, thank you that we are important to you, even if we are not important to others. Amen.

For Discussion: Encourage the child to think of everything she knows about kings. What does he think it would be like to be a king? What would the most special part be? What would the hardest part be?

Activity: With any media at hand, help the child learn about ancient kings. A visit to a museum would be helpful. Be sure to include the Bible's description of kings.

NOTES

David, a Boy

Scripture: 1 Samuel 16:4-13

Memory: 1 Samuel 16:13
Then Samuel took the horn of oil, and anointed him in the presence of his brothers; and the spirit of the LORD came mightily upon David from that day forward. Samuel then set out and went to Ramah.

Memory verse for younger children:
The spirit of the LORD came upon David.

 **Meditation:** It is often difficult to remember that the Lover of All does not look at people as we do. We choose the biggest, richest, brightest, strongest, the most powerful. Our Lord looks at our hearts, and chooses accordingly. The One Who Sees All judges by that which we cannot see. David had a heart for the Lord. We are told nothing about his faith to this point, but we discover later that he trusted God to help him care for his sheep, and he would trust God to help him do whatever it becomes his lot to do. David was apparently pleasing to look at, but he was the youngest of many brothers, and even the seer Samuel expected to pick one of the older boys. This youngest son of Jesse was the one who had a heart like the Lord's and he would become Israel's second king.

 Prayer: I know God looks at my heart and can choose me to do a special work, even though I am young. Thank you, God. Amen.

For Discussion: David was a shepherd. Talk to the child about the things a shepherd might do. How would the child feel if he was chosen as a youngster to be king over many people? Help the child draw parallels and contrasts between caring for sheep and ruling over people.

Activity: (1) Obtain a copy of the book *A Shepherd Looks at the 23rd Psalm*.[1] Use this to help the child discover how caring for sheep can relate to caring for people. (2) If you have any shepherds in your area, visit them and find out about their work.

NOTES

---

1   W. Phillip Keller, A Shepherd Looks at 23rd Psalms (Zondervan, 2008)

David, a Warrior

Scripture: 1 Samuel 17:40-50

Memory: 1 Samuel 17:45
But David said to the Philistine, "You come to me with sword and spear and javelin; but I come to you in the name of the LORD of hosts, the God of the armies of Israel, whom you have defied."

Memory verse for younger children:
"I come to you in the name of the LORD."

Meditation: In this famous encounter, we get a glimpse of David's faith. The people around him wanted to cover him with armor or entirely forbid his entrance onto the field of battle. David had a source of protection and strength that neither his brothers nor King Saul seemed to know about. The giant Goliath saw this youngster coming toward him as an insult. His pride may have caused his downfall. David replaced a sword with five stones, thrown with the skill of one who had often protected sheep from predators. Goliath was only a somewhat larger predator, preying on the Israelites. Goliath's height is described as "six cubits and a span," which would be about nine and a half feet. David, a youth, might have been at least four feet shorter. In David's eyes, the difference was insignificant, because God more than made up for the difference.

Prayer: Lord, sometimes the things I face seem very big. Help me remember that you can help them seem smaller. Amen.

For Discussion: This popular story should be easy to get into. How would you feel if you were in the same situation as David? Would you be afraid? Confident? Faithful? Boastful? What are the people who are watching—including David's big brothers—thinking about what they see?

Activity: (1) Help the child act out this battlefield story. Help him try to put himself in the place of David, Goliath, David's brothers and King Saul. (2) Show the child how tall nine and a half feet would be.

NOTES

David, a King

Scripture: 2 Samuel 2:1-7; 2 Samuel 5:1-5

Memory: 2 Samuel 2:4
Then the people of Judah came, and there they anointed David king over the house of Judah. . . .

Memory verse for younger children:
The people of Judah anointed David king.

Meditation: David was a source of both the division and the reunification of Israel. Much of Israel wanted to follow Saul's family, but it eventually became clear that David was the best choice for both groups. David was of the tribe of Judah, so it was natural for them to be the first to follow him, but eventually all of Israel was united under his rule. If you look at a Bible Atlas, you will see that there is a geographic division: Israel to the north and Judah to the south. Later, the distinctions between these two kingdoms would become quite sharp, but under David's rule, they became one. David continued to care for the remaining family of Saul, mostly because of an oath made to Saul's son Jonathan, whom David loved. Qualities such as his faithfulness endeared the people to David. David was almost always faithful to the Lord, but when he did stray, his repentance was genuine and his relationship with his God was restored.

Prayer: Lord, help me to be the kind of person that others will like. Amen.

For Discussion: Are there people who seem to dislike the child? Encourage the child to talk about this. Help him understand some ways to bring reconciliation with these people. If that doesn't seem likely, encourage the child to treat the others kindly, even if they don't like him.

Activity: (1) Help the child list their strongest qualities. Ask the child if these are things others should like. (2) Help the child list his weaknesses. How should others feel about these? Encourage the child to work on his assets and strengthen his weaknesses.

NOTES

_____
_____
_____
_____
_____
_____
_____
_____
_____
_____
_____
_____
_____
_____
_____
_____
_____

Solomon, a Wise King

Scripture: 1 Kings 3:4-15

Memory: 1 Kings 3:9
"Give your servant therefore an understanding mind to govern your people, able to discern between good and evil; for who can govern this your great people?"

Memory verse for younger children:
"Give your servant an understanding mind."

Meditation: Solomon could have asked for anything, but he asked for understanding, or wisdom. The Eternally Wise One, pleased with this request, gave Solomon two important things he didn't ask for: wealth and power. Although in his prayer Solomon refers to himself as a little child, he was well into young adulthood by the time he succeeds to the throne. He was not David's oldest surviving son, but, as so often happened in Scripture, he was the one chosen for this important position at this time. The Kingdom is united and at peace. Solomon's greatest undertaking was the building of the temple. We see some glimpses of Solomon's wisdom, such as the case of the two women and the baby, but many of these accounts are not provided to us. Instead, we see instances that seem to demonstrate anything but wisdom, such as his marriage to many wives who worship many different gods. The Lord was not pleased with many of the choices Solomon made as his wealth and power grew.

Prayer: Thank you Lord that you help me to make good choices. Amen.

For Discussion: If the child was given an opportunity to have anything she asked for, what would she request? Why did the child make this decision? Help the child think about some choices she has recently made and determine whether these were good or bad choices. Talk about whether or not her choices would please the Lord.

Activity: (1) Solomon's wealth is probably inestimable in today's financial arena. Help the child think about what he would do with unlimited wealth. List these responses in two columns: altruism (helping others) and greed. (2) Encourage the child to do something special for other people, something that requires little or no money.

NOTES

Two Special Prophets

Elijah's Prophecy

Scripture: 1 Kings 17:1-6

Memory: 1 Kings 17:6
The ravens brought him bread and meat in the morning, and bread and meat in the evening; and he drank from the wadi.

Memory verse for younger children:
The ravens brought him bread.

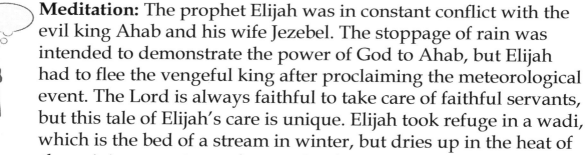

Meditation: The prophet Elijah was in constant conflict with the evil king Ahab and his wife Jezebel. The stoppage of rain was intended to demonstrate the power of God to Ahab, but Elijah had to flee the vengeful king after proclaiming the meteorological event. The Lord is always faithful to take care of faithful servants, but this tale of Elijah's care is unique. Elijah took refuge in a wadi, which is the bed of a stream in winter, but dries up in the heat of summer, thus giving us a time reference for this story. Elijah was able to drink from the wadi. Ravens brought food for the refugee prophet. Ravens are omnivores, eating everything from grain to small animals, but are also carrion eaters, thus causing them to be among the unclean animals. Noah used a raven to help him discover when the waters had dried up. Ravens are one of the animals likely to occupy abandoned buildings and lands.

Prayer: Thank you, Lord, that you care for your children in many special ways. Amen.

For Discussion: Lots of possibilities here: Where did the food come from? Why didn't the bird eat the food? Why did the Lord use an unclean bird, which is not supposed to be touched, to carry the food? Be sure to emphasize that the Lord must have been controlling the bird so that Elijah could be cared for. Why use a bird? Why not make the food just appear, as God did in the wilderness?

Activity: (1) Help the child learn about ravens from a book or museum. (2) Try to visit with a meteorologist to help the child find out about what causes rain.

NOTES

Elijah and the Baal Prophets

Scripture: 1 Kings 18:25-39

Memory: 1 Kings 18: 36

At the time of the offering of the oblation, the prophet Elijah came near and said, "O LORD, God of Abraham, Isaac, and Israel, let it be known this day that you are God in Israel, that I am your servant, and that I have done all these things at your bidding."

Memory verse for younger children:
"You are God. I am your servant."

Meditation: There is a lot of humor in this story, if only in Elijah's taunt to the prophets of Baal. Baal was worshiped by many people of the land as an agricultural god. Israel's King Ahab and his wife had turned away from the true God to worship this pagan idol. Elijah taunts the prophets about their god needing to be awakened, and the prophets increase the intensity of their ritual. Elijah's methods leave no doubt that there is one true God who is able to do all things. The false prophets called upon their idol all day, and were unable to bring down the fire that would demonstrate acceptance of their offering. Elijah then douses his alter and sacrifice with water until the trench usually used to catch the blood from the sacrifice is filled. He does not dance, stab himself or shout, but merely offers a simple prayer, and fire from God came down, consumed his sacrifice and dried up the water in the trench. Once again, God had shown that there was one true Deity, capable of performing marvelous works.

Prayer: Thank you God that you show that you care for your family in many ways. Amen.

For Discussion: Why didn't the Baal prophets get a response from their god? Why did Elijah pour water on his alter three times? Who sent the fire that burned up the sacrifice and the water? Why don't we use dead animals and sacrificial altars today? (Because Jesus became our sacrifice once for all).

Activity: (1) Using whatever media might be available, help the child learn about ancient altars on which sacrifices were made. (2) Talk about miracles, and help the child remember some she may have experienced.

NOTES

_____
_____
_____
_____
_____
_____
_____
_____
_____
_____
_____
_____
_____
_____
_____
_____

God Takes Elijah Away

Scripture: 2 Kings 2:7-14

Memory: 2 Kings 2:11
As they continued walking and talking, a chariot of fire and horses of fire separated the two of them, and Elijah ascended in a whirlwind into heaven.

Memory verse for younger children:
Elijah ascended in a whirlwind into heaven.

Meditation: Elijah, at the prompting of the Lord, had already chosen Elisha as his replacement. We don't know how long the two had traveled together before Elijah was taken away. Elisha asked for a double share of Elijah's spirit, and we see the result of this in his ministry. I think the miracles Elisha did were greater than what Elijah did, and Elisha never ran in fear. The power of God seems more intense in his life. There are two people named in Scripture who never die: Elijah is one, and Enoch is the other (Genesis 5:21-24). The mantle discussed in this passage would have been a square cloth, possibly decorated with fringes, used as an outer garment, wrapped around the body, often for warmth. Elijah's mantle seemed to have special powers which did not end when Elijah was taken away. The powers of this garment might be related to the articles of clothing mentioned in the New Testament which seem to have special powers from the people who wore them. Such ideas are not entirely lost in this enlightened age, as many people value relics or items believed to be possessions of holy people.

Prayer: Thank you, Lord, that you have so many ways to show you care for those you love. Amen.

For Discussion: How did Elisha feel as he watched his friend disappear in the sky? Why did Elisha tear his clothes? Talk about other times when waters had parted and people could walk across on dry land (Exodus 14:21; Joshua 3:15-16).

Read verse 14 and ask the child how Elisha was feeling when he asked where the God of Elijah was. What did he learn?

Activity: Help the child learn about chariots.

NOTES

Elisha Helps a Widow

Scripture: 2 Kings 4:1-7

Memory: 2 Kings 4:5
So she left him and shut the door behind her and her children; they kept bringing vessels to her, and she kept pouring.

Memory verse for younger children:
They kept bringing vessels to her, and she kept pouring.

Meditation: Is this a miracle of oil or vessels? The oil would have been olive oil, common, but also very precious. A room full of filled vessels would have provided for the woman and her children for quite a while. The woman is described as the widow of one of the company of prophets, so this might have been similar to a retirement or death benefit, oriental style. Well-known prophets developed their own following of disciples, who became identified by the prophet they followed. This event shows the compassion of Elisha, and many of the miracles he performs are miracles of mercy. The event which precipitated this miracle was the threat of losing her children to slavery for the collection of debts. This was not uncommon. Children were possessions which could essentially be disposed of as the parents desired, and would be collateral on a debt.

Prayer: Thank you Lord that you provide for us in many different ways. Amen.

For Discussion: What did the woman think as she saw oil continue to pour from her one little bottle? How would the child like to be given to someone as a slave because his parents couldn't pay debts? Would the child like to go around to neighbors and ask for containers?

Activity: (1) Learn about olives and their uses. How do we get the different types of olive oil? (2) Help the child prepare a dish using olive oil.

NOTES

God Heals Naaman through Elisha

Scripture: 2 Kings 5:1-14

Memory: 2 Kings 5:14

So he went down and immersed himself seven times in the Jordan, according to the word of the man of God; his flesh was restored like the flesh of a young boy, and he was clean.

Memory verse for younger children:

His flesh was restored like the flesh of a young boy.

Meditation: There is a lot in this passage. Naaman was not an Israelite, but the commander of an enemy army. We do not know how long he had leprosy. There are a number of skin ailments in Scripture described as leprosy, which may or may not have been. Leprosy is always cleansed. It is never cured or healed. When Naaman is told by his young captive about the prophet in Israel, he gets his king to send a letter to the king of Israel, expecting that he would know of this prophet. The king probably did know of Elisha, but the letter doesn't seem to mention a prophet. The king sees the request as a means of starting a fight. Somehow, Elisha gets word of the predicament and he advises the king in his response. Naaman comes and is told to take a dip in the Jordan River. Nothing to it. Well, Naaman apparently expected a big fuss, and his pride was injured, so he refuses to comply. Only the encouragement of his entourage changes his mind, and when he obeys, he is cleansed.

Prayer: Lord, help me always obey your guidance. Amen.

For Discussion: Would the child do what the prophet said? Talk with the child about diseases or illnesses he has had and how they were cured. Does Elisha's way sound better? Why didn't Naaman want to do what the prophet told him to? What are some examples of times the child finds it hard to obey?

Activity: Look at a Bible atlas and find the land of Aram (Damascus). Then find the Jordan River. Help the child understand how far this general would have traveled to receive his cleansing from his disease.

NOTES

10

The People in a Strange Land

The Holy City Destroyed

Scripture: 2 Kings 25:1 - 3; 8-10; 21b

Memory: 2 Kings 25:21
. . . So Judah went into exile out of its land.

Memory verse for younger children:
So Judah went into exile.

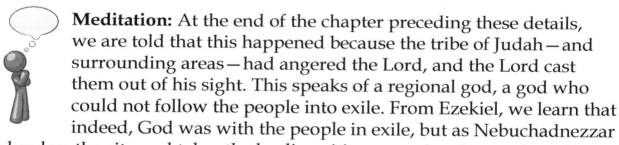**Meditation:** At the end of the chapter preceding these details, we are told that this happened because the tribe of Judah—and surrounding areas—had angered the Lord, and the Lord cast them out of his sight. This speaks of a regional god, a god who could not follow the people into exile. From Ezekiel, we learn that indeed, God was with the people in exile, but as Nebuchadnezzar plunders the city and takes the leading citizens captive, it must have been very difficult to find any trace of God. With few exceptions, the people taken out of the city now are the common people. The main reason Judah displeased God was because they adapted the ways of their neighbors. They worshiped the foreign idols and turned away from the one true God. The exile had the desired effect. Although Israel engaged in many attitudes not pleasing to their Lord, idolatry was never again one of their problems.

Prayer: Lord, we know that sometimes you must respond to our disobedience. Help us to show our love by obeying. Amen.

For Discussion: Talk to the child about the connection between her actions and bad things that happen in her life. Encourage her to talk about her beliefs about God's relationship to this. A child can express eloquent attitudes simply, so listen for the thought behind the words. A connection between actions and consequences may be new for the child, so tread lightly. Help the child understand the importance to the people of all the things in the city that were destroyed.

Activity: (1) Help the child pretend to be leaving his home forever. What things would the child take? What would the child miss most? What concerns does the child have about the new place? (2) Help the child understand the concept of forced removal (exile).

NOTES

A Brave Young Woman

Scripture: Esther 4:1, 4-8, 12-14; 5:1-3, 9-13

Memory: Esther 4: 14
"For if you keep silence at such a time as this, relief and deliverance will rise for the Jews from another quarter, but you and your father's family will perish. Who knows? Perhaps you have come to royal dignity for just such a time as this."

Memory verse for younger children:
"Perhaps you have come to royal dignity for just such a time as this."

Meditation: The book of Esther is a wonderful story of honor and dishonor. The context is many years after the exile, when Babylon, the country which sent Judah into exile, has been conquered by Persia, and the Jews are experiencing more freedom and power than they had under Babylonian rulers. Esther was the "winner" of a contest held to find a queen for the Persian ruler Xerxes. Her uncle Mordecai was honored by the Jewish people but hated by the King's right-hand man Haman. Mordecai's concern in this passage is a decree made by the King, under the influence of Haman, that on a certain day, all the Jews in the land are to be destroyed by their neighbors. Mordecai pressures Esther to go to the King and plead for her people. It is unknown to Haman and the King that Esther is a Jew. Since the King has not called her, she risks her life by approaching the King, but he honors her presence and grants her requests. Because Esther was brave, she saved her people. Mordecai's treachery is revealed, the tables are turned and the King allowed the Jewish people to defend themselves. This event is celebrated today as Purim.

 Prayer: Lord, help me to always be brave like Esther. Amen.

For Discussion: When have you had to be brave? How did you feel? What happened when you were brave? When is it difficult for you to be brave? When is it easy to be brave? Who are your brave heroes?

Activity: Have the child pretend to be Esther, going before the King. What will she do if the King does not acknowledge her? How does she feel when the King offers to grant her request and come to her banquet? How does she feel about Haman, who wants to kill her people? Why does she want Haman to come to her banquet?

NOTES

Three Brave Young Men

Scripture: Daniel 3:1-30

Memory: Daniel 3:18
"But if not, be it known to you, O king, that we will not serve your gods and we will not worship the golden statue that you have set up."

Memory verse for younger children:
"We will not serve your gods."

Meditation: This story takes us back into Babylonian captivity, where King Nebuchadnezzar has erected a statue in honor of himself. At the sound of various musical instruments, all the people are to bow down and worship this idol. Apparently, many Jews refuse to do this. These three young men, Shadrach, Meshach and Abednego, had been given positions of responsibility, and so they were singled out for punishment. They declare that their God may not rescue them, but they still will not bow down to the King's idol. Into the fiery furnace they go! Immediately, a fourth figure is seen in the furnace, a figure that appears as a god. The young men are removed from the furnace, and don't even smell of fire. Suddenly, their God gains great favor, and is proclaimed as the only God who can deliver (people) in this way. No one in the land was allowed to speak a word against the God of Shadrach, Meshach and Abednego. It is believed that the fourth figure in the furnace is a theophany, an appearance of God and possibly even an incarnation of Jesus himself.

Prayer: Lord, help me always to trust and follow you, even if it means people will not be happy with me. Amen.

For Discussion: Help the child understand the differences between the bravery of these young men and the bravery of Esther. The ruler did not listen to their plea, and an attempt was made to put these three to death. Talk about their willingness to die for being faithful to their God. How did God rescue them? Talk with the child about times they may have to stand up for God against others.

Activity: Role playing. Help the child act out the parts of one of the young men, the King, and one person who is watching and sees what happens. How do they respond? What do they say to those around them? Do they want to follow the God of the young men?

NOTES

Daniel is Faithful

Scripture: Daniel 6:10-23

Memory: Daniel 6:22
"My God sent his angel and shut the lions' mouths so that they would not hurt me, because I was found blameless before him; and also before you, O king, I have done no wrong."

Memory verse for younger children:
"My God sent his angel and shut the lions' mouths."

Meditation: The Persian King Darius was persuaded by jealous leaders to make a proclamation that he was to be the only one prayed to (ancient kings were generally seen as gods). This was done in an attempt to discredit Daniel, an exiled Jew. The only "fault" the leaders found in Daniel was that he would not abandon his regular prayer practices, and they used this to trap him. Daniel, as expected, continued to follow his established pattern of prayer, knowing that he would be seen and reported. When the King finds out that Daniel is the one being betrayed, he is heartbroken. Daniel's life had previously made a good impression on him. He is unable, however, to go against the proclamation. Throughout the night, as Daniel faces the hungry lions, the King experiences restlessness, denying his usual evening pleasures. First thing in the morning, he goes to check on Daniel, and finds that he is unharmed, the mouths of the lions having been shut. Daniel was protected because he had trusted in his God.

Prayer: Lord, I want to be like Daniel and always be faithful to you. Amen.

For Discussion: What would the child have done if he were in Daniel's place? Would he stop praying or try to hide his prayers? Talk about having such a life that others are jealous of you. When has the child been jealous of someone? What did they do about their jealousy?

Activity: (1) Read about lions and their eating habits. (2) Go to a zoo and look at lions. (3) Have the child draw a picture of Daniel in the pit with the lions. (4) Have the child draw or tell how he thinks the lions were kept from harming Daniel.

NOTES

Jonah's Strange Journey

Scripture: Jonah 1:1-3, 12, 15-17; 2:1, 10; 3:1-10; 4:1

Memory: Jonah 1: 17
But the LORD provided a large fish to swallow up Jonah; and Jonah was in the belly of the fish three days and three nights.

Memory verse for younger children:
The LORD provided a large fish to swallow up Jonah.

Meditation: The focus of this story is neither the swallowing by the fish nor the prayer inside the fish. The point is Jonah's disobedience and rebellion, even after being vomited by the fish and reluctantly witnessing to Nineveh, the Assyrian capital. Jonah regrets that God has repented and decided not to destroy this heathen stronghold. Jonah's understanding of the God of Abraham, Isaac and Jacob was that only Israel was worthy of salvation. He whines and mopes, and God has to teach him a lesson about arrogance through a worm and a bush. Jonah is not an attractive figure, and I generally don't like teaching this story about one so rebellious. The children can get into the "gross" factor of a man being vomited by a fish, but there are far more important points in this story. God gave Jonah a special mission. At first Jonah tried to run, but that outcome was so unpleasant, that he reluctantly obeys. His obedience is empty, however, as we discover when God spares the city. Jonah preached repentance, and when that is accomplished, he becomes angry. Jonah had much to learn about obeying God.

Prayer: Lord, sometimes I don't want to do what you want me to do, but help me do it anyway, with joy. Amen.

 For Discussion: Why wouldn't Jonah want the Deity to spare Nineveh? What happened inside the fish? How could the Lord command the fish to vomit Jonah up?

Activity: (1) Have the child draw a picture of what Jonah looked like when the fish vomited him up after three days. Would people want to be around him? Why or why not? (2) Find Nineveh on a Bible atlas map. How far is it from the water? How far is it from Tarshish?

NOTES

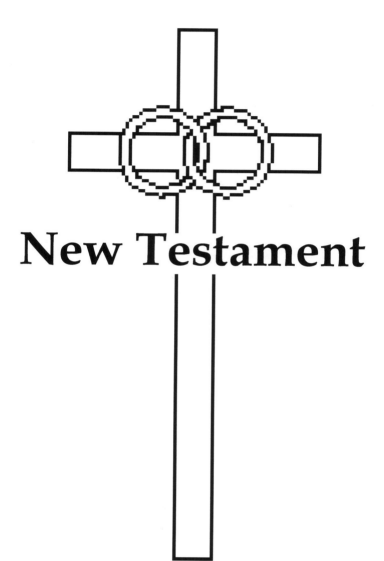

New Testament

1

The Messiah

A Special Baby

Scripture: Luke 2:8-20

Memory: Luke 2: 11
". . . to you is born this day in the city of David a Savior, who is the Messiah, the Lord."

Memory verse for younger children:
". . . to you is born this day the Messiah, the Lord."

Meditation: What a wonderful way to announce the birth of a king: to shepherds, maybe the most humble of workers. Jesus' most common reference to himself is as the Son of Man, but he also refers to himself as the Good Shepherd. He came for all, but his ministry would mostly be to the marginalized, the forgotten, and the lowly. The birth of this Messiah was not announced with fireworks or spectacle that often follows the birth of kings — although the appearance of the angels must have seemed very spectacular to the shepherds. His was a long-awaited birth that was barely noticed by anyone. Mary and Joseph must have wondered about these men and boys who came to the animal shelter where they had to rest and deliver the child. We are told that Mary treasured the story in her heart. As her son grew and began his ministry, as he was beloved by common people, but rejected by the religious leaders, did she think back to this humble beginning? This was the most special birth in the history of humanity, and would result in a life lived as an example to all humanity. But the most significant act of this unheralded child would be his death for all humanity.

Prayer: Thank you Lord that Jesus came for me, under conditions that would be hard for me. Amen.

For Discussion: Talk with the child about the circumstances surrounding his birth. Were a lot of people present? Did the birth happen under any unusual circumstances (e.g., in a car or at home)? How would the child feel about being put in a feeding trough as her first cradle?

Activity: Help the child portray all the factors of this special birth through any media: in an animal shelter; shepherds being addressed by angels; shepherds coming; the baby in a feeding trough (manger); the animals that might be in the shelter.

NOTES

Simeon and Anna Celebrate the Birth

Scripture: Luke 2:25-40

Memory: Luke 2:30
For my eyes have seen your salvation,

Memory verse for younger children:
My eyes have seen your salvation.

Meditation: Simeon and Anna, unacquainted as far as we know, seem to be symbols of so many things: God's reward to those who faithfully serve; God's faithful fulfillment of promises; the gift of discernment of the Holy Spirit, and, for Anna, the significance of women in the Kingdom. These two elderly people did not accidently happen to be at the Temple that day. They were faithful servants, and had awaited the birth of the Messiah. Undoubtedly through the Holy Spirit, both recognized this boy, brought to the Temple to fulfill the requirements of the law, as the Awaited One. Both praised God for the honor of seeing this special child. Both spoke as prophets: Simeon, to the parents of the child, and Anna, to all she came into contact with who had awaited this birth. The child's parents were amazed at what was being said. Had they already forgotten the visits of the angels before the birth and the stories of the shepherds afterwards?

Prayer: Thank you Lord for those who believe what you say. Amen.

For Discussion: How did the Holy Spirit let Anna and Simeon know that this was the Messiah? Why was Simeon now ready to die? Why did Simeon and Anna both praise God? Remind the child of some things people said about him when he was born.

Activity: Using any chosen media, have the child depict the Holy Spirit. How does the Holy Spirit tell people things? What is the child's understanding of whom the Holy Spirit is? Help the child include his answers in his depiction.

NOTES

Visitors From Far Away

Scripture: Matthew 2:1-12

Memory: Matthew 2:1
In the time of King Herod, after Jesus was born in Bethlehem of Judea, wise men from the East came to Jerusalem.

Memory verse for younger children:
Wise men from the East came to Jerusalem.

 **Meditation:** I never put the wise men in the nativity scene at Christmas, because they came significantly later. Apparently Mary and the child are still in Bethlehem, but they are in a house, not the stable. In the Greek, a different word is used for the newborn baby and for this child. These wise men from the east may have been astrologers, who discovered a new star and sought its significance. We are not told how they related the star to the birth of a king, but it was common to relate celestial phenomena to the arrival of royalty. Herod, the current king of Israel, would have expected future kings to come from his family, so imagine his response at having these strangers come inquiring about a newborn king. The amazing part of this story is not the star or the assumptions of the wise men, but the fact that they followed this star and it led them right to the Christ child.

 Prayer: Thank you, Lord, that you guide us in many ways. Amen.

 For Discussion: How did the king feel when these men came looking for a newborn king? What does the child think the wise men looked like? How did they travel? How could they bring such expensive gifts as gold? What did Mary do with the gold and other gifts (it is believed by many that these gifts financed the trip to Egypt to protect the child from King Herod's anger)? Why does the child think a star was used to guide these men from very far away?

Activity: Get some star charts and help the child understand the paths, origins and lives of stars. Help the child find the North Star, which is the largest star in our galaxy, but apparently was dwarfed by the star that led the wise men.

NOTES

The Boy Jesus in the Temple

Scripture: Luke 2:41-51

Memory: Luke 2:49
He said to them, "Why were you searching for me? Did you not know that I must be in my Father's house?"

Memory verse for younger children:
"I must be in my Father's house?"

Meditation: When people traveled long distances, they went in large groups, for safety and company. The Passover was one of the three feasts in Jerusalem which required attendance by at least the men. Imagine this twelve-year-old boy sitting among the Jewish elders and holding their attention. He had apparently been well schooled in the Scriptures to be able to do this. Some questions are raised by this incident: why would he expect his parents to know where he would be? Why did he not tell them where he would be? Jesus had apparently come to a recognition of his relationship with God, the Father that his earthly parents were not aware of. When he tells them he must be in his Father's house, they are confused. Significantly, Jesus is submissive to them, and goes with them obediently. The home study Jesus had done was beginning to pay off. Jesus had learned, not only from any earthly teachers he may have had (we don't know about his childhood study), but he learned from God.

Prayer: Thank you, Lord, that you help us learn in many ways.

Amen.

For Discussion: Talk about some twelve year olds the child may know. Would they be able to sit and discuss Scriptures with adults? How does the child think Jesus got his knowledge? Why were Jesus' parents upset? Why did they not understand what Jesus meant when he said he had to be in his father's house? When is it hardest for the child to obey parents? Has the child ever gotten lost? Tell the child how you felt when you could not find him.

Activity: Help the child find different parts of Scripture: Old Testament, New Testament; different books. Look at different parts of a Bible: maps, the index, concordance. All these things help in learning Scripture. Begin to teach the child the books of the Bible, beginning with the New Testament.

NOTES

John the Baptizer

Scripture: Matthew 3:1-12

Memory: Matthew 3:11
"I baptize you with water for repentance, but one who is more powerful than I is coming after me; I am not worthy to carry his sandals. He will baptize you with the Holy Spirit and fire."

Memory verse for younger children:
"One who is more powerful than I is coming after me."

 **Meditation:** John was distantly related to Jesus, and was chosen by God to prepare the way for Jesus' ministry. He called people to repentance of sin, and many of the common people, along with some religious leaders, responded. Once people had repented of their sin, their hearts were prepared to hear and receive the message of Jesus. While Pharisees and Scribes came for baptism, their future response to Jesus indicates that their hearts were not changed. Apparently John and Jesus did not know each other as children, because John only knows Jesus by the work of the Holy Spirit, and he recognizes him when he sees him. John is a transition prophet: he follows the mold of the Old Testament prophet in his eccentricity, but he is the forerunner of a New Covenant given through Jesus. Ultimately, John baptizes Jesus just as Jesus is about to begin his ministry. John is soon put to death, his work being finished.

 Prayer: Thank you Lord that you call people to help you in your mission to this world. Amen.

For Discussion: Why did the people come to be baptized by John? What did John look like? What did he eat? Would the child eat these things? Talk about what it means to be baptized.

 Activity: (1) Go to a local church that has a baptistry and have the leader of that church explain their baptism guidelines and procedures to the child. (2) Explore with the child other means of baptism in your community: a font used for sprinkling or christening; a lake or river. Perhaps the child could also personally witness a baptism.

NOTES

Jesus Begins His Ministry

His Baptism

Scripture: Luke 3:21-22

Memory: Luke 3:22
And a voice came from heaven, "You are my Son, the Beloved; with you I am well pleased."

Memory verse for younger children:
"You are my Son; with you I am well pleased."

Meditation: Don't all children love to hear these words of encouragement from their parents? Jesus' ministry on earth was only three years, and he was about thirty when it began. Therefore, he had spent many years in preparation for his earthly ministry. We know very little about those years. We are given a glimpse into his life at the age of twelve (Luke 2:41-52), but in Scripture, that is all we are told. There are some extra-scriptural texts that purport to talk about his childhood, but we really can only speculate. However, it is clear from the Father's words that Jesus had led a life that was indeed pleasing to the Father. Hebrews 4:15 tells us that Jesus was without sin, so many of the childhood "vices" such as lying, stealing, or worse, would seem to be absent from his life. Now, as Jesus is about to begin his ministry, the Father expresses his love for and pleasure with this young man, providing all parents with an example that should be followed often. Children who receive such expressions of love and encouragement grow with the ability to express such affirmation to others.

Prayer: Lord, thank you that my parents love me. Help me to learn to love and encourage others. Amen.

For Discussion: How did Jesus feel when he heard these words come from heaven? Do you think the other people heard these words? Would it be scary to hear words from the sky?

Activity: (1) Work with the child to help him list ways in which he feels that his parents love him. As you do this, discuss with the child the things you do for and with the child because you love him. (2) As you do things with the child, hug and hold him close. (3) Schedule a "Love Day" where only love words will be spoken and love actions demonstrated.

NOTES

The Temptation

Scripture: Luke 4:1-12

Memory: Luke 4:1
Jesus, full of the Holy Spirit, returned from the Jordan and was led by the Spirit in the wilderness.

Memory verse for younger children:
Jesus was led by the Spirit in the wilderness.

Meditation: Jesus had just experienced a high point of his life through his baptism. Now, the Spirit leads him into the wilderness to be tempted by the devil. The Son's success in the face of these temptations would determine his success throughout his ministry. Any temptation we might face is encompassed in the three temptations Christ faces: the desire for provision; the desire for power and the desire for love and popularity (the people would see him on the pinnacle and admire his courage for jumping). Jesus responds to every temptation by quoting Scripture, which he had learned throughout his life. The devil acts as if he does not know that Jesus is Lord over all things, and that nothing can be given him that is not from the heavenly Father. This temptation is only one of the reasons the devil is called the father of lies. Jesus demonstrates not only his knowledge of Scripture, but also his faithfulness to the Father and the mission for which he was sent. He faced temptations that all humanity faces, but on a greater scale. He did not give in to the temptations and demonstrated his worthiness to become the Son of Man and the Savior of all humanity.

Prayer: Protector, help me when I face temptations to do wrong things. Help me be strong. Thank you, Amen.

 For Discussion: Why did the devil think Jesus would want bread? What would it feel like to rule all the kingdoms of the world? Why didn't Christ do what the devil wanted him to do?

Activity: (1) Help the child identify things that tempt him to do the wrong things. Some possibilities: friends; seeing something someone else has but we don't; thinking that we should do what we want. (2) As you watch TV or movies, help the child identify things that tempt people, and discuss how they resist or give in.

NOTES

Teaching in Nazareth

Scripture: Luke 4:14-30

Memory: Luke 4:28
When they heard this, all in the synagogue were filled with rage.

Memory verse for younger children:
All in the synagogue were filled with rage.

Meditation: The activity described in this passage is typical of Jewish worship of Jesus day: the Scriptures were read and then discussed. Jesus first tells the people that the Scripture he has read is fulfilled, that he is the one upon whom the Spirit of the Lord rests. The people of Jesus' hometown can accept this. They are really impressed by his understanding, since he is just the son of a local carpenter, Joseph. Then Jesus starts to talk about existing conditions in the days of the prophets Elijah and Elisha, but only two foreigners, the woman of Sidon, and Naaman the Syrian, were ministered to. The people of Nazareth, being Jews, believed that they were the only ones worthy of God's healing ministry, so they were offended that Jesus would point out these examples. He also seems to be saying that the Lord's favor was not upon the people of Nazareth, and so they quickly change from admiration to rage, and want to kill him for pointing out truths. Very often, when we begin to follow God, the people who are closest to us, those who know us the best, will not understand or accept the work the Lord begins to do in our lives. This was the case with Jesus, as even his own family did not understand.

Prayer: Help me, Lord, to understand that people will not always understand my desire to follow you. Amen.

For Discussion: Why could Jesus do miracles in some places, but not in others? Why did the people want to kill Jesus? What would you do if people wanted to kill you? How do you think Jesus got away?

Activity: (1)Talk with the child about times when people do not seem to understand the good things she does. (2) Help her understand that the motives behind what we do have to be pleasing to God, as well as the actions we take. (3) Talk with the child about motives.

NOTES

Healings

Scripture: Luke 4:38-44

Memory: Luke 4:40
As the sun was setting, all those who had any who were sick with various kinds of diseases brought them to him; and he laid his hands on each of them and cured them.

Memory verse for younger children:
He laid his hands on each of them and cured them.

Meditation: Word of the healing of Peter's mother-in-law must have spread quickly from this house, which probably became Jesus' Capernaum home. The fever which was healed would have been severe, perhaps accompanied with other symptoms such as dysentery. After the healings, Jesus went off by himself. This text says the crowds looked for him; Mark tells us that Peter and other disciples looked for him. All were impressed with the healings and wanted Jesus to continue. Healings were important to Jesus' ministry, but they were not the most important thing. Jesus had a temporal ministry to the people of his day, but his primary mission was the proclamation of the Kingdom of God. Signs such as healing, provision and resurrection of people like Lazarus supported this mission. Jesus also had a mission which helps all people throughout eternity. This was the ministry of salvation, and he performed this ministry when he surrendered his sinless life to cover the sins of all on the cross.

Prayer: Lord, thank you that Jesus helps me in many different ways. Amen.

For Discussion: How do you think people felt when they were healed by Jesus? What would you do if Jesus healed you?

Activity: If the child is old enough to understand, talk to him about Jesus dying on the cross. Otherwise, help the child understand other ways in which Jesus helps: providing food, shelter, loving parents, good friends, opportunities to learn, healing, and comfort. Ask the child about ways in which he thinks Jesus helps him.

NOTES

Calling Helpers

Scripture: Mark 3:13-19

Memory: Mark 3:13-14
He went up the mountain and called to him those whom he wanted, and they came to him. And he appointed twelve . . .

Memory verse for younger children:
He appointed twelve.

Meditation: That Jesus called twelve people to himself is important for us in many ways. First, those who follow Jesus today are descendants of those early disciples. Next, the disciples demonstrate many human shortcomings, showing us that we don't have to be perfect to follow Jesus. Next, that Jesus chose twelve followers makes it obvious that we are not intended to serve by ourselves. Finally, the calling of twelve disciples expresses the idea of discipleship. When we come into God's Kingdom, we can't grow and survive on our own. We need to be taught, and we need to be teachers. These twelve men followed Jesus everywhere, except into his quiet moments of prayer and onto the cross. They observed his compassion and ministry to others. They saw the examples of peace, comfort and strength in the face of oppression and hostility. All that Jesus represented was available for his followers to see, and, after Jesus ascends to heaven, we see the Holy Spirit working in their lives to duplicate Jesus' life within them. The Holy Spirit works in the lives of Followers today, teaching and helping us to live the life of Jesus, and helping us help others to know the life of Jesus.

Prayer: Lord, please teach me to be one of your disciples. Amen.

For Discussion: What would you do if Jesus asked you to follow him? Did Jesus know that Judas, one of his disciples, would betray him? How do you think Jesus treated Judas, whether he knew of his betrayal or not? How can Jesus help you to help others?

Activity: (1) Help the child recognize people who have taught her: Sunday school teacher, day care worker, school teacher, parent, big brother or sister. (2) Identify some of the things she has been taught. (3) Help the child write a thank-you note to one of her teachers.

NOTES

3

Teachings and Examples

Love Your Enemies

Scripture: Luke 6:27-35

Memory Verse for all children: Luke 6:31

Do to others as you would have them do to you. [This is called the Golden Rule]

Meditation: These words of Jesus are often difficult to hear. It is not easy to return good for bad, and often the offender would not even accept our offer of good, believing there to be some hidden motive. The modern idea of lending implies a return, so we might better understand what is being talked about here as gifting. Give whatever is asked of you, expecting no return. This is a hard concept to hear. We are called to live above the norm. The "catch" is that we can only do this through the power of the Holy Spirit. When we allow the life of God to live through us, then we can live as Jesus, loving those who demonstrate anything but love toward us, but that is the only way we can do this. When we try to comply with this admonition of Jesus apart from the power of the Spirit, we end up doing so with wrong motives or only partially fulfilling the command. Chances are that the child has already experienced the hostility of others. How he hears and responds to these words will give you good insight into his heart.

Prayer: Lord, help me to be like you and turn the other cheek. Amen.

For Discussion: Do you think anyone hates you? How do they treat you? How does Jesus want you to treat them? Is following Jesus' words hard or easy?

Activity: (1) Help the child identify behaviors that would indicate that someone does not like her. (2) Have the child describe a behavior that would please Jesus, according to our passage today. Help the child reflect on whether or not she would really be willing to do these things or whether she already does them.

NOTES

_____

_____

_____

_____

_____

_____

_____

_____

_____

_____

_____

_____

_____

_____

_____

_____

The Samaritan Woman

Scripture: John 4:4-15; 21-26; 28-30

Memory: John 4:14
"But those who drink of the water that I will give them will never be thirsty. The water that I will give will become in them a spring of water gushing up to eternal life."

Memory verse for younger children:
"The water that I will give will become in them a spring of water."

Meditation: There are cultural concepts in this story that will be foreign to the modern American reader: prohibitions against a man and woman interacting in public; a Jewish man with a Samaritan woman; and a man of good reputation with a woman of bad reputation. As you share this passage with the child, bring out the ironies and activities that might be more understandable to her life: Jesus asks for water, then says that he will give the woman living water; Jesus himself is the Living Water; the woman speaks of Messiah and Jesus is the Messiah; Jesus is giving us a good example of how to witness to others. This is a very important story about relationships in Scripture. It supports Jesus' teachings about how we are to treat our enemies. Because Jesus took the time and opportunity to minister to this woman, her life was changed, the lives of many people in her community were changed, and we are given an example of loving our enemy.

Prayer: Lord, help me to love others as you love me. Amen.

For Discussion: What does Jesus say about water in this passage?

What does Jesus mean when he talks about "living water?" The community this woman was part of was an enemy to Jesus people. Do you think Jesus treated this enemy in a good way?

Activity: (1) Have the child draw pictures of people who might not like him. Then have the child draw how he should treat these people. (2) Have the child draw the description Jesus gives of living water.

NOTES

Eight Special Blessings

Scripture: Matthew 5:3-10

Memory: Matthew 5:9
"Blessed are the peacemakers, for they will be called children of God."

Memory verse for younger children:
"Blessed are the peacemakers."

Meditation: These familiar blessings are called the Beatitudes, and, like many of Jesus' teachings, they are not always easy to understand or follow. What does it mean to be "poor in spirit?" How do we know when we are being meek? What does "pure in heart" mean to a child? Not in this text, but in several other places, Jesus gives us the answer. We will look into the answer more thoroughly later, but for now we will look at the answer in relation to these admonitions: Jesus says we must be like children. Children are uncomplicated, not sophisticated, and as such will inherit the Kingdom of heaven. Children have a wonderful sense of humility (meekness). The innocence of children relates to pureness of heart. Unfortunately, children of today are exposed to many things that may quickly rob them of the attributes of which Jesus speaks. When we think about the attributes of children, we must think of children untarnished by the electronic, the abuser, the neglecter, and the weaknesses of today's educational system, to name a few. Look at this text from the point of view of the child's understanding, guiding but not insisting.

Prayer: Lord, help me to help others find peace in you. Amen.

For Discussion: Which of these blessings do you like best? How can you do what it says? Do you know people who demonstrate these qualities?

Activity: Help the child prepare a chart with eight columns. Put one of these blessings at the top. Under the blessing, put the result. Under each one, put the child's idea of what is meant. Then help the child identify (1) people who he thinks demonstrate each quality, and (2) ways that the child can demonstrate each quality.

NOTES

Give to the Needy

Scripture: Matthew 6:1-4

Memory: Matthew 6:3
"But when you give alms, do not let your left hand know what your right hand is doing."

Memory verse for younger children:
"Do not let your left hand know what your right hand is doing."

Meditation: The implication here is that of a theatrical performance, an idea that matches our idea of hypocrisy: giving in such a way as to make sure people see and appreciate what you are doing, even to the extent of blowing a trumpet to get attention. Jesus is talking about people who love the praise of others. All they can expect is public acclaim and praise. There will be no eternal reward. To "give alms" is to do a charitable deed. Jesus tells us that we are to give without drawing attention to ourselves and without trying to get the recognition of others. In this way, our gifts for others will be recognized by the heavenly Father, who will reward us. The eternal reward is not so much for how much we give but for the attitude of our hearts as we give. Our gifts are to be so secret, not even the hand opposite the one with which we give is to know about our gifts. The promise here is also one of secrecy. As we give in secret, so we will be rewarded in secret. People shouldn't know about what we give, and they shouldn't know about the way the Holy One rewards us for giving.

Prayer: Lord, help me to always give some of what I have to those in need. Amen.

 For Discussion: When you do good things, do you like people to see what you do? Do you tell people about good things you do? How can you help people who do not have as much as you do?

Activity: (1) Find a community project which helps needy people, and help the child get involved in this in some way. (2) Talk to the child about different ways he might draw attention to himself. (3) Help the child understand right motives in doing things.

NOTES

Praying

Scripture: Matthew 6:6-14

Memory: Matthew 6:8
"Do not be like them, for your Father knows what you need before you ask him."

Memory verse for younger children:
"Your Father knows what you need."

Meditation: The place of prayer here is a place where the world can be shut out and you can commune with the Lord in privacy. The idea of secrecy is emphasized, because the religious leaders of Jesus time would stand in public, beat themselves on the chest in mock humility and make sure that people around them heard and saw their piety. Like those who publicized their giving, these receive their reward in their recognition by others. We are admonished not to babble or use vain repetitions. This does not mean we cannot use meaningful repetitions in our prayers, because Jesus himself repeated the request for the cup to pass three times in Gethsemane just prior to his crucifixion. A pagan concept of prayer was that many repetitions would weary the gods and get the desired result. Jesus speaks elsewhere of persistency, but what matters is the attitude of our hearts and the sincerity of our words. Jesus then goes on to instruct his followers how to pray, in what we call the Lord's Prayer. He offers a model for prayer, offering several elements. I don't think Jesus intended that this particular prayer should become a source of rote ritual, prayed meaninglessly week after week.

Prayer: Dear Lord, please teach me how to pray as you would. Amen.

 For Discussion: Do you like to pray? What kind of things do you pray for? Have you ever had a prayer answered? Do you like to pray with other people or by yourself?

Activity: There are several elements of prayer in the Lord's Prayer: petition (asking for things); praise of God; a wish for God's will; a wish for God's protection; a request for forgiveness. Take each of these and help the child understand each one, applying them to the child's life and understanding.

NOTES

Greatest in the Kingdom

Scripture: Matthew 18:1-6

Memory verse for all children: Matthew 18:4
"Whoever becomes humble like this child is the greatest in the kingdom of heaven."

Meditation: These words must have come as quite a shock to Jesus' listeners. Children were possessions, nonentities in the culture of Jesus' day. How can such beings be the greatest in the Kingdom of heaven? In another setting, two of Jesus' disciples were arguing about which would be at his right hand and which at the left in the Kingdom. No humility there! When we welcome children into our churches, into our lives, into our hearts, we welcome Jesus. When we put stumbling blocks before children, we will receive a harsh penalty.

What might some modern stumbling blocks be?

- Anything that will discourage a child.
- Anything that harms a child and causes anger, bitterness or any other negative attitude within the child.
- Anything that prevents a child from growing in a healthy, strong manner.
- Anything—such as movies and video games—that teaches a child attitudes that are not the attitudes of Jesus.
- Anything that deprives a child of his natural birthrights of humility, innocence, curiosity, trust, acceptance and love.

Children are gifts given to us to teach us how to get ready to be part of the heavenly Kingdom.

 Prayer: Lord, help me teach grownups how to be like a child. Amen.

For Discussion: How does it feel that Jesus thinks that the greatest in the Kingdom are just like you? Do you know what it means to be humble? How can you help grownups be like you? How do you think grownups should not be like you?

Activity: (1) Help the child identify characteristics of children that might have been special to Jesus (some are listed above). (2) Help her identify which ones she has and does not have. (3) Talk to the child about how she might become more like the children Jesus was talking about.

NOTES

The Lord's Supper

Scripture: Matthew 26:26-30

Memory: Matthew 26:26-27
While they were eating, Jesus took a loaf of bread, and after blessing it
he broke it, gave it to the disciples, and said, "Take, eat; this is my body."
Then he took a cup, and after giving thanks he gave it to them, saying,
"Drink from it, all of you."

Memory verse for younger children:
"Take, eat; drink from it, all of you."

Meditation: How you approach this passage will depend on
the age and experience of the child. If the child has not been
baptized as a believer or confirmed, they may not be taking
communion in church yet. However, they can start understanding
the significance of this important memorial to Christ. While we
can do a "learning" Eucharist, we should never make light of
this special meal. Before a child takes communion, he should understand
the significance of the meal; that it is not just a snack that grownups take
periodically. In these elements, there are pictures of Jesus. Jesus is the
Bread of Life (John 6:35 & 48). He also tells us that he is the Vine (John
15:5), referring to the grape vine from which wine comes. In the Eucharist,
the bread represents his own body, which is about to be crushed. The
wine is his blood, which seals the new covenant he is about to enact. Jesus
offered himself up for us, and encourages us to remember him every time
we partake of these elements. We should take this meal with sorrow,
remembering what he had to go through for us. But we should also

celebrate with joy and thanksgiving that he was willing to make such a sacrifice.

 Prayer: Lord, thank you for offering your body and blood for me and my family. Amen.

 For Discussion: What does the bread mean? What does the wine/juice mean? What other ways can you remember Jesus?

Activity: (1) If the child is not yet taking communion in church, be sure that they are present some Sunday when the meal is served. (2) Prepare a "learning" meal for the child, consisting of some grain product (crackers, cookies) and grapes. Help the child understand what each element represents. Be sure the child understands why they may not be receiving the meal in church.

NOTES

Miracles of Jesus

A Dead Girl Lives Again

Scripture: Luke 8:41-42; 49-56

Memory: Luke 8:53
And they laughed at him, knowing that she was dead. But he took her by the hand and called out, "Child, get up!"

Memory verse for younger children:
He called out, "Child, get up!"

 **Meditation:** There are some beautiful parallels between these passages and the passage which is sandwiched by them. While Jesus is on the way to heal the twelve-year-old daughter of Jairus, another woman intercepts him. This woman has had an issue of blood for twelve years, and had been socially dead. The woman is healed by her faith, after she touches Jesus. The girl is healed by the faith of her father and the touch of Jesus' hand. In each case, Jesus confronts the onlookers, first to ask who touched him, then to rebuke those who are mourning the girl. At the touch of Jesus' hand and the sound of his voice, a child who had been dead came to life. Her parents were astonished, and were probably overwhelmed with joy, and yet they were directed by Jesus to say nothing. How would you respond to observing the miracle of seeing your child brought back from the dead? Jesus was Life, and he bestowed life, whether literally or socially, throughout his ministry. These two stories demonstrate the full spectrum of Jesus' mission.

 Prayer: Lord, thank you for the special ways in which you showed love and demonstrated the powers of God. Amen.

For Discussion: Do you think it would be scary to die? What do you think the little girl did when Jesus healed her? What would it sound like if Jesus spoke to you? What would it feel like to be touched by Jesus?

Activity: (1) Help the child understand death, through whatever media you feel would be most helpful for the child. (2) Read about the resurrection of Jesus (Matthew 28:1-8), and help the child understand that because Jesus lives, we can live.

NOTES

Feeding 5,000 People

Scripture: Mark 6:32-44

Memory: Mark 6:37
But he answered them, "You give them something to eat." They said to him, "Are we to go and buy two hundred denarii worth of bread, and give it to them to eat?"

Memory verse for younger children:
"You give them something to eat."

Meditation: In this popular story, we see the compassion, authority, power and sufficiency of Jesus. He took five loaves of bread and two fish, food that might have fed one family, and fed thousands of people. This story could be seen as Eucharistic, as a picture of the breaking and blessing of the bread, portrayed in the Last Supper (Luke 22:19). The thing I like most about this story is that Jesus is not only distributing food for the people, but he is distributing himself. Matthew 6:35 tells us that Jesus is the Bread of Life. This story is a demonstration of the sufficiency of Jesus for all people. Through modern-day disciples of Jesus, each person can receive Christ, just as each person on the hillside that day received food. There was no partiality, as the food was distributed to all who were present, and all can receive Jesus today. The grace of God pours through Jesus in great abundance, represented by the excess of food on that day. This story not only represents the literal feeding of people, but the spiritual sufficiency of Christ for every need.

Prayer: Thank you, God, that through Jesus we can have all we need. Amen.

 For Discussion: How do you think Jesus made enough bread and fish to feed so many people? Why was there so much left over after everyone was fed? Do you think Jesus' helpers knew that he was doing a miracle?

Activity: (1) Help the child learn about the food in Jesus' day. (2) Help them make some bread that looked like the ancient bread which Jesus shared with others.

NOTES

Healing a Man who can't Move

Scripture: Mark 2:1-12

Memory: Mark 2:5
When Jesus saw their faith, he said to the paralytic, "Son, your sins are forgiven."... Mark 2:11 "I say to you, stand up, take your mat and go to your home."

Memory verse for younger children:
"Take your mat and go to your home."

Meditation: Roofs on the homes in Jesus day were flat and often the scene of family activity, so breaking through a roof and lowering a mat to Jesus would not have been as difficult as it might be today. There are several thought-provoking pictures in this story. First of all, it is the faith of the man's friends that seem to spark the interest of Jesus and his healing response. Does this mean that the faith of our friends can bring healing to us? Secondly, the first thing Jesus does is forgive the man's sin. The common belief of the day was that sin caused illness, poverty and many of the other woes of humanity. Jesus forgave the man's sin, something the bystanders could not see, but he also healed his body, something all present could see. In the eyes of pious Jews, the physical healing of the man was a sign of his spiritual healing. In between the two events, Jesus seems to be aware of the thoughts of the teachers who are present. The healing of the man's body almost seems to be a response to the hardheartedness of the onlookers. In the end, all were amazed and went away praising God, which should always be the result of seeing the work of Jesus.

Prayer: Lord, thank you that you care for all of us, our bodies, minds and souls. Amen.

For Discussion: Why did the man's friends carry him to see Jesus? Would you do what they did for a friend? How do you think the man felt when he picked up his mat and carried it home? How do you think his friends felt?

Activity: (1) Help the child learn about the types of houses in Jesus' day. (2) Have the child act out the story with other family members, portraying the different parts: sick friend, helpful friends, teachers and Jesus.

NOTES

Walking on Water

Scripture: Mark 6:45-51

Memory: Mark 6:48
When he saw that they were straining at the oars against an adverse wind, he came towards them early in the morning, walking on the sea. He intended to pass them by.

Memory verse for younger children:
He came towards them early in the morning.

Meditation: Jesus performs several miracles in this story: walking on water, calming the storm and calming the disciples. He was able to do these things because he had spent time in prayer. Because Jesus was fully man as well as fully God, prayer recharged him and prepared him for whatever would come. It can do the same for us. Jesus' times of prayer always came at very crucial points in his ministry. This time on the water immediately followed the feeding of the 5,000, a miracle which probably drained Jesus of his spiritual strength. Prayer enabled him to continue and help his disciples. Why were the disciples afraid when they saw Jesus? Ghosts were a very real thing for the people of Jesus' day. The Age of Enlightenment has deprived humanity of belief in things like ghosts, for the most part, but to many cultures, spirits of the deceased are very real. The disciples in the wind-blown boat did not see their Lord and Master. They saw the afterlife remains of an unnamed person. Once they realized that the specter was Jesus, once they heard his voice, once he got into the boat with them, all was well. Jesus can bring this same kind of peace to us. There is a song with lyrics that say "sometimes he calms his child, sometimes he calms the storm." Even if Jesus does not calm our storms, he can walk with us through them.

Prayer: Thank you, Lord, that you are always near to us and we never need to be afraid. Amen.

For Discussion: Have you ever seen a ghost? Would you be afraid of a ghost? What things make you afraid? Can Jesus help you not be afraid?

Activity: (1) Talk with the child about storms she has experienced. What scared her about these storms? (2) Have the child draw a picture of this story, including all elements: Jesus in prayer; the storm; the boat and the men in it; Jesus on the water; the storm being quieted; the peace of the disciples with Jesus in the boat.

NOTES

Calming a Storm

Scripture: Luke 8:22-25

Memory: Luke 8:24
They went to him and woke him up, shouting, "Master, Master, we are perishing!" And he woke up and rebuked the wind and the raging waves; they ceased, and there was a calm.

Memory verse for younger children:
And he woke up and rebuked the wind.

Meditation: Although this story is similar to the one where Jesus walks on water, there are some important differences: (1) Jesus starts out in the boat with the disciples; (2) Jesus goes to sleep; (3) Jesus rebukes the disciples and the elements, and (4) most of the fear of the people comes *after* Jesus has calmed the storm. Jesus, who created the elements that were assaulting him and the men, had power over those elements, but once again, his followers did not seem to know who he was. The little nap Jesus took was interesting. Was it a test? Was he just plain tired? Did he know the storm was coming? The men in the boat were experienced fishermen, and a storm would not usually present too much of a challenge. Water could be bailed out. Perhaps they were just a little annoyed because Jesus was sleeping and ignoring their plight. When Jesus calms the storm, it doesn't seem to calm the men in the boat. In fact, they seem to have a negative response to Jesus' words and actions. Maybe they had as difficult a time dealing with his rebuke about their lack of faith as they did with his nap in the face of danger. Seeing someone speak to wind and water and get a response would probably be frightening to anyone who doesn't understand the source of the power.

 Prayer: Even in the face of scary things, I thank you, Lord, that you are with me. Amen.

For Discussion: Why do you think Jesus went to sleep? What things made the men afraid? What do you think Jesus said to the wind and the rain? What do you think these men said to their families when they got home?

Activity: (1) Let the child play with a toy boat in a bathtub or sink. Create some waves and wind (hand motions/fan). (2) Help the child understand some of the things the men on the Lake faced as water filled the boat. (3) Talk about their fear and how Jesus stopped the storm.

NOTES

Raising Lazarus

Scripture: John 11:1-6; 14-17; 21-27; 32-35; 41-44

Memory: John 11:43
When he had said this, he cried with a loud voice, "Lazarus, come out!"

Memory verse for younger children:
He cried with a loud voice, "Lazarus, come out!"

Meditation: We aren't told about many people actually being loved by Jesus, so Mary, Martha and Lazarus were very special to Jesus. Certainly, if Jesus had gone to Bethany earlier, he could have healed Lazarus, so by waiting until he knows Lazarus is dead, he is trying to demonstrate the power of God and to demonstrate that he is indeed the way, the truth and the life (John 14:6). When Martha meets Jesus, her words seem harsh and condemning. When Mary comes, her words are the same as Martha's, but her attitude is different: she knelt at his feet and she was weeping. Then, as he is being shown where the deceased Lazarus had been laid, Jesus himself begins to cry. He was not only feeling the pain of the two women, but experiencing his own pain and, perhaps, is getting a picture of what he is soon to experience in his own death. There is no doubt that this was a highly emotional experience for Jesus. As Jesus gives the command for Lazarus to come from the grave, Jesus specifically addresses Lazarus. Some have suggested that if Jesus had not spoken Lazarus' name, every person who had ever died would come back to life. Whether or not that is true, we have here an incredible representation of the power and authority of the Living Word.

Prayer: Thank you, Lord, that you can comfort me even in very hard times. Amen.

 For Discussion: What does it feel like to be dead? Why did Jesus bring Lazarus back to life? What happened to Lazarus after he was brought back to life?

Activity: (1) Take the child to an old cemetery and look at many of the gravestones, remarking on the inscriptions. (2) Have the child express his feelings about what some of these people and their families must have been like.

NOTES

5

Jesus' Last Days

People Want to Kill Jesus

Scripture: John 11:46-53

Memory: John 11:53
So from that day on they planned to put him to death.

Memory verse for younger children:
They planned to put him to death.

Meditation: Jesus had become a thorn in the side of the religious leaders of his day. Even though Jesus helped a lot of people, the religious leaders thought that he was a threat to their position and the security of Israel, their nation. The raising of Lazarus was probably the final straw. As the leaders gathered to begin in earnest the effort of planning Jesus' death, the high priest prophesies that one person must die so that the whole nation can be saved. Caiaphas could not have known how true this prophecy was, yet in a way he could not have understood or intended. Jesus would die, not only for the nation of Israel, but for all people of all places of all times. It is difficult to think about Jesus having to die, but it is through his death that we can know reconciliation with God, forgiveness of our sins and eternal life. As the leaders of Israel gathered, they inadvertently began planning for the fulfillment of what God had ordained from the foundation of the world. These religious leaders felt that they followed God, but in this instance, it would be beyond their imaginations to imagine how closely they were fitting into God's eternal plan.

Prayer: Lord, I don't like to think of Jesus dying for me, but I thank you that he was willing to do so. Amen.

 For Discussion: What are some things Jesus did that made the leaders want to kill him? How do you feel about Jesus dying? Why did God plan for Jesus to die?

Activity: (1) Talk with the child about the reason Jesus had to die, e.g., to redeem people from their sins (Review Genesis 2:15-25). (2) Have the child name some things in their life that they think might be sins. (3) Have them ask Jesus to forgive them for these sins. (4) Encourage the child to portray how they feel knowing that Jesus forgives their sin.

NOTES

Entering Jerusalem

Scripture: John 12:12-19

Memory: John 12:13
So they took branches of palm trees and went out to meet him, shouting, "Hosanna! Blessed is the one who comes in the name of the Lord-- the King of Israel!"

Memory verse for younger children:
Blessed is the one who comes in the name of the Lord.

Meditation: This is the story of the day we have come to call Palm Sunday, the Sunday before Easter. This is Jesus' final entry into Jerusalem, although he does make one or two brief trips outside the city gates. Jesus rode a donkey, which David, Israel's greatest king, also rode. Because of the palm branches, some think this entry occurs during the Festival of Booths, but the different texts clearly indicate that Passover, the celebration of the liberation from slavery in Egypt, is at hand. Many of the people in Jerusalem are pilgrims who have come from other nations to celebrate the Passover. Some may never have seen or heard of Jesus. As a crowd gathered, many of these pilgrims possibly joined in, heard the stories of Jesus and the rumors, and welcomed the one who came as a new King. Most of the people expected Jesus to rule as an earthly King led by God, to set them free from the rule of the Roman Empire. Jesus would be a King, but he would hold no earthly throne. Jesus came to be King of the hearts and lives of people, but those who greeted him that day did not understand this. They wanted freedom and peace, which would come from Jesus, but not in the way the adoring crowds expected. Hosanna, blessed is the One who comes in the name of the Lord!

 Prayer: Lord, help me to make Jesus king of my heart and life. Amen.

For Discussion: Why were the people so happy to see Jesus come riding into Jerusalem? Today, if we saw a king, would we see him riding a donkey? What would a king ride in today? How would the people who served the King show that they were glad to see him?

Activity: (1) Using some visual media, have the child depict Jesus entry into Jerusalem. Discuss the presence of things like garments on the ground, the palm branches, happy people and the donkey. (2) How would the child depict Jesus as a King?

NOTES

Betrayed By Judas

Scripture: John 18:1-11

Memory: John 18:2
Now Judas, who betrayed him, also knew the place, because Jesus often met there with his disciples.

Memory verse for younger children:
Judas betrayed him.

Meditation: Judas Iscariot had been a follower, or disciple, of Jesus for about three years. He was the treasurer of the group (John 13:29). We really don't know why Judas turned Jesus over to the authorities for 30 pieces of silver (Matthew 26:15). Was he disappointed that Jesus was not going to rule as Judas expected him to when he began following him? Did he think that once Jesus was arrested, Jesus would stop the death process by calling down angels and taking over? I don't think Judas really expected Jesus to die. Judas was part of God's plan for the redemption of the world, but he was still held responsible for his actions (Luke 22:22). The Gospel writer Matthew tells us that Judas hanged himself as a result of his betrayal (Matthew 27:5). John seems to be the harshest of the evangelists on Judas. He describes him as a thief (John 12:6) and as one destined to be lost because of his betrayal of Jesus (John 17:12). John is the only one who has Judas complaining about Mary's use of expensive ointment to anoint Jesus (John 12:4-5). The other gospel writers indicate objections voiced by others, possibly more than one. Judas betrayed Jesus with a kiss (Matthew 26:49; Mark 14:45), using an act of love to indicate to Jesus' apprehenders whom they should arrest. Earlier in the evening, at the meal shared by Jesus and his disciples, Jesus had shown love to Judas by washing his feet (John 13:5), even though he knew of his intended betrayal.

 Prayer: Dear God, please help me always be loyal to Jesus. Amen.

For Discussion: Why did Judas turn Jesus over to the people who wanted to kill him? How did Jesus treat Judas when he knew he would betray him? How would you have treated Judas if you knew what he was going to do? If you were one of Jesus' friends, how would you treat Judas after Jesus was arrested?

Activity: Have the child depict what he thinks Judas looked like (1) when Jesus chose Judas to be one of his followers; (2) when Jesus was washing his feet; (3) when he kissed Jesus in the garden so the mob would know who to arrest; (4) after Jesus was sentenced to death.

NOTES

Denied by a Friend

Scripture: Matthew 26:69-75

Memory: Matthew 26:75
Then Peter remembered what Jesus had said: "Before the cock crows, you will deny me three times." And he went out and wept bitterly.

Memory verse for younger children:
"You will deny me three times."

Meditation: Matthew is the only evangelist (gospel writer) who puts all three of Jesus' denials in one place. John and the others seem to indicate that the denials took place in two different places, as Jesus was taken from one place to another for his trial. Regardless, Jesus had predicted Peter's denial (John 13:38, Matthew 26:34, Mark 14:30, and Luke 22:34). I don't think there is any doubt that Peter really loved Jesus, and later, after Jesus' resurrection, Peter would become one of Jesus' most faithful followers. At this time before the crucifixion, Peter is acting out of fear and the need for self-protection. He rightly feels that his life is in danger, which is what is controlling his responses to this dark situation. Tradition tells us that later Peter indeed lays down his life for Jesus, but right now, he is not yet ready to do that. Peter doesn't just say that he doesn't know Jesus. At one point, Peter becomes quite vehement in his denials (Matthew 26:74). Afterward, Peter must have felt that it was all over, that he had failed his Lord completely. Peter wasn't at the cross. He didn't see Jesus die, but he was one of the first to see the empty tomb. If he thought that Jesus was alive, he probably assumed that Jesus would want nothing to do with him. Scripture tells us that Jesus appears to Simon Peter on that Resurrection Day (Luke 24:34) but we are told nothing of the details of that special meeting. We can only know from future actions of Peter that Jesus restored Peter's faith and peace.

Prayer: Lord, sometimes I say things I don't mean. Help me to think about everything I say. Amen.

For Discussion: Why did Peter say that he didn't know Jesus? Would you ever say that you did not know someone who was special to you? How did Peter feel? Have you ever felt sad because you said something that hurt someone else?

Activity: Talk with the child about ways we protect ourselves when we think we are in danger. Let the child depict some of these things in her chosen media. Have the child think about how some of these self-protective ways might hurt someone else. Talk about which the child thinks is more important: self-protection or not hurting someone.

NOTES

Crucifixion

Scripture: John 19:23-30

Memory: John 19:30
When Jesus had received the wine, he said, "It is finished." Then he bowed his head and gave up his spirit.

Memory verse for younger children:
Jesus bowed his head and gave up his spirit.

Meditation: We attribute seven different sayings to Jesus on the cross. Three are depicted in today's passage. Others are: "Father, forgive them" (Luke 23:34); "My God, My God, why have you forsaken me?" (Matthew 27:46); "Into your hands I commit my spirit" (Luke 23:46) and, to the thief who hung on the cross beside him, "This day you will be with me in Paradise" (Luke 23:43). Of these seven expressions, three relate to other people: the people who are crucifying him; his mother and a beloved disciple; and the repentant thief. If we were in the same situation, would we be thinking of the well-being of others? It's true, Jesus did think about his own needs, as he experienced separation from the Father, thirst and the presence of death, but I tend to think that is all most of us would be thinking about. It was very likely Jesus' compassion for others, expressed in the context of such an agonizing situation, that caused a centurion who had probably been instrumental in Jesus' crucifixion to proclaim, as Jesus died, "truly, this man was God's son" (Matthew 27:54). Surely, the crucifixion of Jesus was unlike the crucifixion of any other person. As Jesus died, some phenomena were present that had probably not been experienced during a previous crucifixion: midday darkness (Matthew 27:45); the temple curtain was torn in two, the earth shook (Matthew 27:54) and graves were torn open (Matthew 27:52). It was truly a momentous occasion, but the best was yet to come.

 Prayer: Lord, I am sorry Jesus had to die, but thank you that he was willing to do so for me. Amen.

 For Discussion: If Jesus was God and could have protected himself, why did he die? Why did Jesus feel that God had left him? Why did Jesus give his mother to a disciple?

Activity: (1) As much as is appropriate for the child's age, do some research on crucifixion as capital punishment by the Romans. Help the child understand that the crucifixion of Jesus was part of God's plan (Galatians 3:13). (2) Talk about what it may have been like for Jesus' mother and others who loved him to watch him die.

NOTES

_____
_____
_____
_____
_____
_____
_____
_____
_____
_____
_____
_____
_____
_____

The Empty Tomb

Scripture: John 20:1-9

Memory: John 20:9
For as yet they did not understand the scripture, that he must rise from the dead.

Memory verse for younger children:
He must rise from the dead.

Meditation: This was early in the morning of the third day after his family and friends had watched Jesus die: the day Jesus died was the first day; from sunset of that day to sunset of the next was the second day; sunset of the second day began the third day. What a dark time it had been in the hearts of those who loved Jesus! No one seemed to remember the things Jesus had said about rising from the dead (Matthew 16:21). Their hope was gone. Now, to add to their agony, the body had been removed from the grave. Who could be this cruel? The women who came to make the final burial preparations were the first to hear the words "He is not here, he has risen" (Luke 24:5) from the angel at the tomb. It was Mary Magdalene, one who had been set free from demons and had been faithful in following Jesus, who was the first to see the risen Jesus (Mark 16:9). He appeared at some point to Peter alone, then to two disciples who were returning home to Emmaus (Luke 24:13ff) and finally to all the disciples as they hid in the Upper Room (John 20:19). What a celebration! Peter especially, who had denied knowing Jesus, must have reveled in the grace and peace of the risen Savior. They could touch him, talk with him, watch him eat and receive his peace. Jesus was not dead! He lives! Soon, Jesus would ascend to heaven, to resume his place with God, the Father, who had commissioned him for his earthly mission, now complete. He would leave the disciples, but he would not leave them alone. Jesus told his followers to wait, and they did. They had to wait about 50 days, but the result was well worth the time.

 Prayer: Lord, I am so glad Jesus is alive! Thank you. Amen.

For Discussion: How would you have felt if you had found an empty burial place? Would you be angry or sad? Would you believe it if someone told you they had seen Jesus after he died? How would you feel when you saw Jesus? What would you want to tell Jesus?

Activity: (1) Have the child depict the empty tomb, the angel(s) at the tomb, the women who first found the stone rolled away, and the disciple who saw the empty wrappings that had been around the body of Jesus. Let the child describe each of these to you. (2) Let the child depict Jesus after he arose from the dead.

NOTES

The Beginning of a New Church

Jesus Sends the Holy Spirit

Scripture: Acts 2:1-15

Memory: Acts 2:4
All of them were filled with the Holy Spirit and began to speak in other languages, as the Spirit gave them ability.

Memory verse for younger children:
All were filled with the Holy Spirit.

Meditation: Jesus had ascended back to heaven, and he instructed his followers to wait for the Advocate to come. One hundred twenty people gathered in Jerusalem, waiting to see what would happen. Could they have imagined a heavenly wind inside the building, tongues like flames, and speaking in unknown languages? No wonder many of the people who heard them as they went out into the street thought they were drunk. Three thousand people believed in Jesus on that day. This is the day of the Festival of Pentecost, a harvest festival about 50 days after Passover. Like Passover, many pilgrims were in Jerusalem to celebrate this required festival. Some may have remembered the dark events of the Passover Festival—the trial and crucifixion of a popular preacher named Jesus—but these things were probably new to most. And now they hear the story in their own languages. I have always considered this to be a miracle of hearing as much as of speaking, but one thing is sure: the followers of Jesus were speaking known languages, although the language was not known to them. They were not speaking some secret, totally unknown language. As "tongues" developed in the growing church, the Spirit may indeed have given a new, unknown language as proof of the belief of new followers. God can use any method, known or unknown, to teach the gospel message to those called to the Kingdom.

   Prayer: Lord, thank you that you chose a special way to help people learn the message of Jesus. Amen.

For Discussion: Why do you think God used different languages to speak to the people? Why did the people in Jerusalem think Jesus' followers were drunk? How do you think that Jews came to live in so many different parts of the world?

Activity: (1) Look at a Bible map or other ancient map and find the countries represented by all the people in Jerusalem. (2) Have the child depict what the "tongues of fire" looked like as they rested on the believers.

NOTES

_____
_____
_____
_____
_____
_____
_____
_____
_____
_____
_____
_____
_____
_____
_____
_____
_____
_____
_____

Fellowship

Scripture: Acts 2:42-47

Memory: Acts 2:42
They devoted themselves to the apostles' teaching and fellowship, to the breaking of bread and the prayers.

Memory verse for younger children:
They devoted themselves to the apostles' teaching and fellowship.

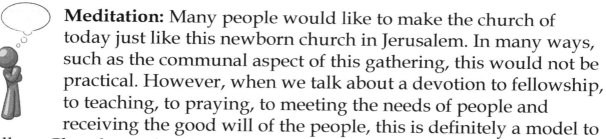

Meditation: Many people would like to make the church of today just like this newborn church in Jerusalem. In many ways, such as the communal aspect of this gathering, this would not be practical. However, when we talk about a devotion to fellowship, to teaching, to praying, to meeting the needs of people and receiving the good will of the people, this is definitely a model to follow. Churches today that are providing food, clothing, shelter, other life assistance and education for people who need those things are the churches that are gaining the good will of their communities and are growing. Unfortunately, this idyllic situation did not last long. Dissension soon rears its ugly head among the believers. We hear more and more about their disagreements and less and less about their fellowship and about the wondrous miracles they were able to perform in the name of Jesus. Today, fellowship in the church has come to mean little more than getting together for food. Fellowship is all the benefit we share together in the name of Jesus. We are called to fellowship with God and with others who believe in God, and the more things we do together as the church, the better we live within this fellowship.

Prayer: Thank you Lord that we can be part of your fellowship with others when we go to church. Amen.

For Discussion: What things do you think the people of the early church did when they got together? Why did the early church have the goodwill of the people? Why do you think that God brought new people into the church every day?

Activity: Have the child depict some of the attitudes and practices of the people in this early church. This might include things like joy, freedom from fear, peace, helping others, learning about Jesus, and sharing all of their things.

NOTES

Peter Heals a Beggar

Scripture: Acts 3:1-10

Memory: Acts 3:6
But Peter said, "I have no silver or gold, but what I have I give you; in the name of Jesus Christ of Nazareth, stand up and walk."

Memory verse for younger children:
"In the name of Jesus, stand up and walk."

Meditation: This wonderful little story tells us that God is still at work through the members of the new church. Actually, I think God is still in the business of doing miracles, but we have had the belief in such miracles educated out of us. It all began in what is called the Age of Enlightenment. We are now an enlightened people who aren't supposed to believe in such things as miracles. Pity! Wouldn't it be wonderful to say to someone crippled by disease or accident "stand up and walk" and to believe and know that as God worked through us, we could see such a miracle? Talk about being able to help people! I do believe God still heals through the prayers of God's people, but these are more or less isolated incidents and don't receive the notice they should. I love the account of the joy of this man after he is able to walk. Imagine the man's surprise as Peter took his hand and helped him on his feet that had never worked properly. He is leaping, walking with others to church and, most importantly, praising God. No rehab, no walking lessons. Just the free and easy ability to get around like anyone else. The resulting amazement of the people probably led to more people joining the church that week.

Prayer: Thank you, Lord, that you still do miracles. Please help us to believe. Amen.

For Discussion: How do you think the man felt when he could not walk? How did he get money? How do you think Peter knew he could help the man walk? How did the man feel after he could walk? Why were the people in the town so surprised?

Activity: This is a great story for a "before" and "after" depiction. Help the child be sure to include things like the man's pastime, being carried into the temple (church) and the amazement of the crowd.

NOTES

Philip and the Ethiopian

Scripture: Acts 8:26-40

Memory: Acts 8:30
So Philip ran up to it and heard him reading the prophet Isaiah. He asked, "Do you understand what you are reading?" He replied, "How can I, unless someone guides me?" And he invited Philip to get in and sit beside him.

Memory verse for younger children:
"Do you understand?" "How can I, unless someone guides me?"

Meditation: This is a story about one of the foreigners who came to worship in Jerusalem, much like the festivals of Passover and Pentecost. He has a scroll and is reading from the prophet Isaiah. The texts which we now identify as the Old Testament were the only Scriptures in existence at that time. The passage he is reading is one that has now been identified as a Messianic text, a text that predicts the coming of the Messiah. Jesus is believed to be the fulfillment of these texts. When Philip asks the man if he understands, the man indicates the need for help. Philip jumps onto the chariot and begins to interpret the texts for him. This text offers a wonderful opportunity for telling the gospel message of Jesus, and Philip doesn't overlook that opportunity. Philip must have taken the story all the way to being baptized in the name of Jesus, because as they approach water, the Ethiopian requests baptism. Philip is able to fulfill this request, and another believer is added to God's Kingdom. As they come up out of the water, Philip is snatched away by God's Spirit, and the Ethiopian goes on his way rejoicing. His life has been changed because of his belief in Jesus! As he returns to his native land, he certainly told of what he had heard and learned. Other people would have believed and thus the church of Jesus Christ continued to grow. This is the way Christianity spread around the world. **Note:** A eunuch is a person who has been neutered, but it is also the title of court officials in the ancient Middle East.

 Prayer: Thank you Lord that people still tell the story of Jesus. Amen.

For Discussion: Why did God send Philip to meet this man? What was the man in the chariot reading? Why do you think he did not understand? How did Philip get to tell the man the story of Jesus? What did the man want to do after he heard the story of Jesus?

 Activity: (1) Find Ethiopia, Gaza and Jerusalem on a map and help the child understand the distances involved. (2) Look up pictures of ancient chariots (probably Egyptian would be the closest).

NOTES

A New Leader

Scripture: Acts 9:3-16

Memory: Acts 9:5
He asked, "Who are you, Lord?" The reply came, "I am Jesus, whom you are persecuting."

Memory verse for younger children:
"I am Jesus, whom you are persecuting."

Meditation: When we last saw Saul, he was holding the clothes of those who were stoning Stephen, the first martyr of the Church, giving approval to his murder, and persecuting the church (Acts 7:58; 8:1-3). Saul thought that people who followed Jesus did not love God, and so he made it his mission to arrest followers of The Way and send them to trial. When Saul encountered Jesus on the road to Damascus, Saul was probably very surprised to hear Jesus talk to him, but it definitely made an impression on him. People in the church were very afraid of Saul, so it is easy to understand the reluctance of Ananias to pay a visit to the persecutor of the faithful. It seems to have taken quite a while for Saul to develop the trust of the church, but eventually he is accepted. His name is changed to Paul, he became one of the most faithful church planters, and many of our New Testament texts were written by Paul. Help the child understand that sometimes, when we are really wrong about an attitude or belief, Jesus can help us change our minds.

Prayer: Dear Lord, thank you for helping me see when I have a bad attitude and helping me change. Amen.

For Discussion: Do you think Saul was frightened when the light and sound from heaven came? Would you be frightened? Why were people afraid of Saul? How did Saul feel when he couldn't see? What do you think happened in the three days that Saul could not see?

Activity (1) Look at a Bible map and find the road from Jerusalem to Damascus. (2) Help the child depict changes in Saul: his appearance; his attitude; his new faith in Jesus. (3) Show Saul with some of his new friends.

NOTES

Peter's Special Dream

Scripture: Acts 10:9-23

Memory: Acts 10:13
Then he heard a voice saying, "*Get up, Peter; kill and eat.*" But Peter said, "By no means, Lord; for I have never eaten anything that is profane or unclean."

Memory verse for younger children:
"Get up, Peter; kill and eat."

Meditation: This story reminds us that growing in our faith is always an ongoing process. Peter had been changed at Pentecost, and had become a great leader of the church, but he was still dealing with some of the old laws. We see the evidence of two depicted in this story: the rule against eating unclean food and the tradition of not associating with Gentiles. Through his command to eat the unclean food animals in the sheet, the Holy One is trying to help Peter learn to accept new things. Three times the sheet is lowered and Peter is commanded to eat. Three times Peter refuses. As Peter was trying to figure out what this could mean, he receives a visitor. The Lord told Peter he was to welcome these Gentile visitors. Peter welcomed them and went with them the next day, opening a new era in the life of the infant church. Paul is the main minister to the Gentiles, but Peter now knows that God welcomes all into his family, and wants us to welcome and accept all people.

Prayer: Dear Lord, help me to accept all people as bearing your image and acceptable to you. Amen.

For Discussion: What were some of the animals in the sheet that was lowered for Peter? Would you want to eat some of these things? Help the child understand what it might mean to be in a trance. Are there any people that you do not want to be around? What would Peter have said to the man who came to his house if God had not given him this dream? What does God want you to do if you think you shouldn't be friends with some people?

Activity: (1) Have the child depict the sheet with the various animals. (2) Talk about how Peter believed that only Jews were God's people, and that it was unclean to associate with those who were not Jews.

NOTES

Peter's Escape from Prison

Scripture: Acts 12:1-11

Memory: Acts 12:7
Suddenly an angel of the Lord appeared and a light shone in the cell. He tapped Peter on the side and woke him, saying, "Get up quickly." And the chains fell off his wrists.

Memory verse for younger children:
"Get up quickly."

 **Meditation:** The time that many of the followers of Jesus feared had arrived. Herod, the ruler of the land, killed James, the brother of John, both of whom were original disciples of Jesus. Seeing that this pleased the Jews who were threatened by the Church, he had Peter arrested, planning to put him to death. Peter was thrown into jail, which would have been little more than a cave. Imagine Peter's surprise when an angel appears, taps him on the side, and causes his irons to fall from him. Peter didn't know what was happening, but followed the angel out of the jail. After the angel departed, Peter went to the house where the disciples were enclosed behind locked doors. The people in the house were sure Peter had been put to death. The young woman who answered the door was so excited to hear Peter's voice that she ran to tell the others, without opening the door. They did not believe her, but thought that Peter's ghost must have appeared. Imagine their joy at seeing Peter free and alive!

 Prayer: Thank you Lord that you watch over your children to protect them. Amen.

For Discussion: What was it like to be in jail alone? What would you do if you saw an angel or a ghost? Why did the king want to kill Peter and the others who loved Jesus? Why were Peter's friends so happy to see him?

Activity: (1) Have the child visually depict Peter in jail. (2) Let the child describe the various emotions depicted in this story: sadness; fear; doubt; joy.

NOTES

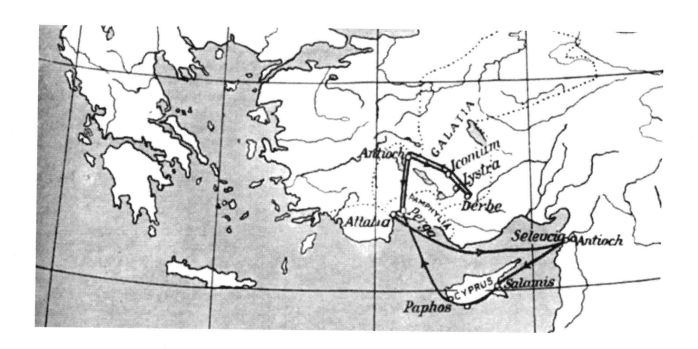

Paul's Missionary Travels

Barnabas and Saul (Paul) Commissioned

Scripture: Acts 13:1-3

Memory: Acts 13:2

While they were worshiping the Lord and fasting, the Holy Spirit said, "Set apart for me Barnabas and Saul for the work to which I have called them."

Memory verse for younger children:
"Set apart for me Barnabas and Saul."

Meditation: The name Barnabas means "son of consolation" or "son of encouragement" and he lived up to his name.

When Saul was in a state of preparation for ministry, learning about Jesus one on one, he lived apart from and not accepted by the Church. Barnabas, from the church at Jerusalem, had gone to Antioch to investigate reports of Greeks being converted to Christianity. When he saw how the Lord was working in that area, Barnabas set out to find Saul and bring him to Antioch. It was in this place and at this time that followers of Christ were first called Christians (Acts 11:26). It was through Barnabas' encouragement that Saul, renamed Paul, became active and accepted in the church. His ministry to Gentiles was more acceptable to the church because of the experience of Peter and the vision of the sheet. Barnabas and Paul traveled together for some time, sharing the gospel of Jesus Christ and planting churches throughout the world. The Lord brought them together, and the Lord sent them out to serve.

Prayer: Lord, help me go wherever you might send me. Amen.

For Discussion: Talk about some of the hazards and difficulties of taking trips in a time when there were no cars, buses, trains or planes. Would you like to travel on a boat to tell people about Jesus? Do you have a friend like Barnabas who helps you feel good about yourself?

Activity: (1) A good Bible map will help you and the child trace the missionary journeys of Paul throughout the Middle East. (2) Help the child plan a trip on a boat. What will he bring? How will he plan his route? (3) Talk with the child about what it means to encourage others.

NOTES

Paul Called Far Away

Scripture: Acts 16:6-10

Memory: Acts 16:9
During the night Paul had a vision: there stood a man of Macedonia pleading with him and saying, "Come over to Macedonia and help us."

Memory verse for younger children:
"Come over to Macedonia and help us."

Meditation: This story reveals the guidance provided by the Lord to Paul. The Spirit makes it clear that they are not to go to two places: Asia and Bithynia. When they are in Troas, Paul then has a dream about a man in Macedonia, calling to them to come to Macedonia. Paul, certain that this is direction from the Lord, makes plans to go to Macedonia, where they first arrive at Philippi. A church is established there. Why was Paul forbidden to go to Asia? Eventually, the gospel is carried to the eastern part of the world, but that would not be Paul's job. If we were to give testimony of such direct guidance by the Lord in our lives today, chances are our witness would be ridiculed and rejected. Why don't we hear about the spirit of the Lord giving us irrefutable guidance and direction? This is a beautiful story, and we should never discount any possibility where the Lord is concerned. If we can do all things through Christ who strengthens us (Philippians 4:13), doesn't it follow that Christ can do all things through us, including give direction and guidance?

Prayer: Thank you, Lord, that you guide and direct me. Help me listen. Amen.

For Discussion: Have you ever heard God tell you anything? What would you do if you did? Do you think God has a plan for where God wants you to go and what God wants you to do? Do you think God could speak to you in a dream?

Activity: (1) "Coincidence" is maybe not a word we should use if we believe in Jesus. Help the child chart events in his life — and yours — that might be considered "coincidence." Review these events and discuss with the child whether or not she thinks these events might be God's guidance. (2) Find Macedonia and Philippi on a Bible map.

NOTES

_____
_____
_____
_____
_____
_____
_____
_____
_____
_____
_____
_____
_____
_____
_____
_____
_____
_____
_____

Singing in Jail

Scripture: Acts 16:25-34

Memory: Acts 16:25
About midnight Paul and Silas were praying and singing hymns to God,
and the prisoners were listening to them.

Memory verse for younger children:
Paul and Silas were praying and singing hymns.

Meditation: The prisoners, and possibly the guard, in this
Philippian jail were listening to these two missionaries because
the missionaries themselves were prisoners. Silas was now Paul's
ministry partner. Paul and Silas had been arrested because they
had set a young girl free from demons, and the men that had
been making a profit from her demon-granted prophetic abilities
dragged them into the town square and had them arrested. Regardless of
this dark situation, Paul and Silas could sing because of the joy of the Lord.

When the earthquake happened, the guard could see only that the doors
were opened. The dark cave did not allow him to see that the prisoners
had not fled, so Paul provided this information. Escape by the prisoners
would have cost the guard his life, so his gratitude is appropriate. He may
not have fully understood what happened, but somehow he discerned that
Paul's God had been responsible. Apparently, this guard had heard some
of Paul's testimony about Jesus and being saved. Later, his entire family
was baptized into the Church of Jesus Christ. Because Paul and Silas had
not become dejected, had continued to trust the Lord and had done the

right thing, the Lord added more souls to the Kingdom.

Prayer: Lord, help me always to be joyful, even when bad things are happening. Amen.

For Discussion: What would you do if you were thrown in jail? Would you be singing? If the doors of the jail were thrown open, would you try to get out? Do you think the jailer was surprised when the prisoners did not run away? Why did the guard at the jail ask Paul what he had to do to be saved?

Activity: (1) Is there a small local or county jail that you might be able to visit? If not, try to meet with someone who works at a jail. Talk about some of the events in this story: (a) Do people sing and praise the Lord in jail? (b) What would an earthquake do? (c) If doors were opened, would prisoners run away? (2) If the child understands "being saved," talk about this event in the child's life.

NOTES

God Protects Paul

Scripture: Acts 18:9-11

Memory: Acts 18:10
"For I am with you, and no one will lay a hand on you to harm you, for there are many in this city who are my people."

Memory verse for younger children:
"No one will lay a hand on you."

Meditation: The city of which the Lord speaks is Corinth, where Paul remains for a year and a half. In Corinth, Paul, who may not have had a missionary partner at this time, met Aquila and Priscilla. This husband and wife were believers and also tentmakers, as was Paul, so they worked together. Silas and Timothy came together to see Paul at Corinth. Corinth was a city of Jews and Greeks and Paul brought the gospel to both. When the Jews (probably Pharisees) opposed Paul's ministry, he determined to preach exclusively to Gentiles. This did not free Paul from persecution, however. He was brought before authorities in Corinth, but was released by a sympathetic proconsul, Gallio. Throughout his travels, Paul would face many court trials, but he did not fear. Much like Jesus, Paul seemed to have a sense about when the time of his departure from this life would occur. He could give free witness to the gospel of Jesus, because he had the promise of God that he would be protected, until it was time for his ministry to end.

Prayer: Thank you for protecting faithful servants. Amen.

For Discussion: What kind of things are you afraid of? Do you think God knows when you are afraid? How can God help you not be afraid?

Activity: (1) Talk with the child about religious differences, especially Christian and Jews. Help the child understand that at one time, Christians and Jews were one group, but separated. Eventually Christians came under the protection of the Roman Emperor Constantine, but Jews have always faced persecution. (2) Introduce the child to different religions that are in our country today.

NOTES

After A Shipwreck

Scripture: Acts 28:1-6

Memory: Acts 28:3
Paul had gathered a bundle of brushwood and was putting it on the fire, when a viper, driven out by the heat, fastened itself on his hand. When the natives saw the creature hanging from his hand, they said to one another, "This man must be a murderer."

Memory verse for younger children:
"This man must be a murderer."

Meditation: Paul was on his way to Rome, to face the Roman emperor. He was a well-treated prisoner, because facing the Emperor was his choice. As the ship on which they traveled faced wreckage due to a storm, guidance given by Paul saved the lives of all aboard. They arrived safely at the island of Malta and were greeted warmly by the people of Malta. A poisonous snake bites Paul, and his death is imminent. Such a death immediately marks Paul as a man who had done wrong, and violent death is his punishment. Judgment soon turns to praise, when it is obvious that Paul isn't going to die. The Maltans go to the other extreme and treat Paul like a god. Paul demonstrates the gospel by healing the father of a leader on the island. Had he not had the experience with the viper, Paul probably would not have gotten close to the ruler. This healing led to many others. We are not told that Paul spoke the message, but sometimes deeds speak a lot louder than words.

Prayer: Dear God, help me show people I love you by the way I live my life. Amen.

 For Discussion: What would you do if a snake bit you? Why did the people think Paul was a bad man? Why didn't Paul die? How did Paul help the people?

Activity: (1) Find the island of Malta on a map. Then find Rome. Talk about how Paul and his traveling companions may have gotten from Malta to Rome. (2) Look at pictures of snakes. Help the child distinguish between poisonous and nonpoisonous snakes. (3) Using a first-aid kit, talk about what to do for a snake bite.

NOTES

Special Teachings

Be Different

Scripture: Romans 12:1-2

Memory: Romans 12:2
Do not be conformed to this world, but be transformed by the renewing of your minds, so that you may discern what is the will of God-- what is good and acceptable and perfect.

Memory verse for younger children:
Do not be conformed to this world.

Meditation: The idea of sacrifice is not a popular one these days. Because God was willing to sacrifice his own son, Jesus, it seems appropriate that a sacrificial life will please God. Sacrifices used to consist of the slaughter of sheep, goats, rams and birds. Jesus fulfilled the need for sacrifices by his own death on the cross.

Now, we are asked to surrender our lives as a living sacrifice. God is not interested in our death, but in how we live our lives. This sacrifice is demonstrated by living in a way that is different from those who do not know the Lord. We are not to conform to the world, but we are to renew our minds, and we do this through disciplines such as scripture reading, meditation on the teachings of the Lord and prayer. When we have renewed minds, we will better be able to know what God's will is for our lives. We will be able to distinguish between things that please God and things that do not.

Prayer: Dear Lord, help me to live my life differently from those who do not know you. Amen.

For Discussion: How do you sacrifice something? What is a living sacrifice? If you could have a new mind, how would it be different? Is God happy with the things you think about? How can you get to know God better?

Activity: (1) Read about ancient sacrifices. All sacrifices are for religious purposes. Read about biblical and non biblical sacrifices. Help the child understand that sacrifices were made to get the deity to do something. (2) Help the child begin to learn practices such as praying and scripture reading that will help transform his mind. For non readers, begin reading daily sections from a children's bible.

NOTES

Love

Scripture: Romans 12:9-13

Memory: Romans 12:9
Let love be genuine; hate what is evil, hold fast to what is good;

Memory verse for younger children:
Let love be genuine.

Meditation: If there is any term that escapes description and definition, it is love. Ask fifty people what love is, and you may get fifty different definitions or descriptions. In our passage today, we are given a list of characteristics of the Christian life, and the list is topped by love. The other characteristics demonstrate love, love for our Lord and love for others. Love is the standard of the Christian life. It is the greatest of all characteristics (1Corinthians 13:13). Many things have been done in the name of love that have nothing to do with love. Jesus commanded us to love the Lord and love one another (Matthew 22:37-39), so we know love isn't a feeling over which we have no control. We choose to love because God first loved us. As you discuss love with your child, listen for attitudes that describe his experience. Encourage the child to understand that the greatest demonstration of love was Jesus' death on the cross.

Prayer: Dear Lord, please help me love other people. Amen.

For Discussion: What is love? How do you show someone you love them? Whom do you love? How do you know when someone loves you? Who are some people who love you?

Activity: (1) Read 1 Corinthians 13:4-7, the "Love" chapter in the New Testament. Help the child understand what each description means. (2) Help the child discover some ways to show love to people within and outside of the family. (3) Talk with the child about the way she feels when she knows someone loves her. Help her depict this feeling with the media of choice.

NOTES

What is Love?

Scripture: 1 Corinthians 13:4-8, 13

Memory: 1 Corinthians 13:13
And now faith, hope, and love abide, these three; and the greatest of these is love.

Memory verse for younger children:
The greatest of these is love.

 **Meditation:** This chapter of Paul's letter to the church at Corinth was written to people who were in disharmony. Paul was trying to show them how those who claimed the name and knew the love of Jesus Christ should act. When we look at these brief descriptions of love, we will recognize that some of these ideas are not commonly accepted. For example, "love endures all things." How often do we hear reports of a criminal act that has been committed against a family member, because the perpetrator was fed up with the victim's behavior? Then, we might hear declarations of love by the perpetrator. Maybe it would have been better if Paul had just come out and said "love doesn't hurt another," but it probably wouldn't make any difference. The common, acceptable definitions of love don't fit God's definitions of love. These words are often repeated at weddings, but they are valuable for every arena in the Christian life, and well worth memorizing.

 Prayer: Lord, thank you that Jesus is a good example of how to love. Amen.

For Discussion: Discuss each element of verses 4-8 with the child, making sure they understand what things like patience, envy, rudeness and resentment mean, within their ability to understand. The child's ideas might be different from yours. Don't impose your definitions on the child, but guide their understanding.

Activity: (1) Using the elements of this passage, encourage the child to discuss times when they haven't been loving. (2) Help the child identify their strengths and their weaknesses within this list. (3) Have the child depict representations of people showing love to others.

NOTES

Righteousness, Peace and Joy

Scripture: Romans 14:16-18

Memory: Romans 14:17
For the kingdom of God is not food and drink but righteousness and peace and joy in the Holy Spirit.

Memory verse for younger children:
The kingdom of God is righteousness and peace and joy.

 **Meditation:** In ancient times, one's religious excellence was demonstrated by how well he kept the festivals, seasons and other external signs of religion. This passage is Paul's attempt to revise that attitude. Maybe the people in the Church of Rome were partying too hardy, thus the admonition to not let their good be spoken of as evil. The Kingdom of God isn't about how well we do the externals. It is about how well we allow the life of God to work in and through us. This life of the Spirit within will be manifest in external ways, such as ministry, mission and worship, but the external should not be the focus. God is always the focus. A local church that is filled with people who know the righteousness, peace and joy of the Lord is a church that is doing the work of God in its community and around the world.

 Prayer: Lord, help me allow Jesus to live his life within me. Amen.

 For Discussion: What is joy? Whom do you know who is always joyful? What is peace? How do you know when someone is peaceful? Where does righteousness come from? Who helps us be righteous?

Activity: (1) Help the child understand what righteousness, peace and joy mean, using a Bible dictionary. Provide the child with examples through people the child knows. (2) Help the child determine ways to fulfill each of these three characteristics. Keep a chart of ways the child has demonstrated these characteristics, offering small rewards for each event.

NOTES

God makes us Special

Scripture: Ephesians 2:10

Memory: Ephesians 2:10
For we are what he has made us, created in Christ Jesus for good works, which God prepared beforehand to be our way of life.

Memory verse for younger children:
For we are what he has made us.

Meditation: Children need to know that they are special to God. When we truly understand that God made each of us through our mommies and daddies, we can better receive the love of God. When we believe in Jesus, we become a new creation, one made to live a life of good works. Children should know that they can do good deeds for others, and that they don't have to wait to be a grown-up. When we learn how precious we are in the sight of God, it helps us realize how special other people are. Doing good deeds for others is a result of recognizing all that God has done for us. Help the child understand that because she has believed in Jesus, her life takes on a very special nature, and should be a life of doing good things. When we do good things for others, we are also doing those good things for God.

Prayer: Thank you, Lord, that I have been created for a special purpose through Jesus. Amen.

For Discussion: Why did God create us? What are some good things we can do for others? How can Jesus help us do good things? How can we show our love for God?

Activity: Help the child remember things that others have done for him. Help the child make a list of good things he can do for others. Help him determine things that can be done alone, and the things he might need help with. Encourage the child to do things without expecting any thanks or recognition. Encourage the child to do at least one thing a week for someone else, especially someone outside of the family.

NOTES

Peace in Jesus

Scripture: Ephesians 2:14-18

Memory: Ephesians 2:14
For he is our peace; in his flesh he has made both groups into one . . .

Memory verse for younger children:
He is our peace.

Meditation: In the early church, there were two groups of people: those who were of the family of Israel, known as Jews, who had followed God through the Law of Moses, and believed in Jesus; and Gentiles, those who learned about God by *hearing* the message of Jesus. Both groups came to worship in the new church, and sometimes there were conflicts. Paul knew that those who followed Jesus should live in peace. Ultimately, all people who believed in Jesus came to be called by other names, such as Believers, Followers of the Way or Christians, and the division of Jew and Gentile in the church disappeared. Now, the word "Jews" took on an additional meaning. Jews were those who didn't believe in Jesus, and Christians and Jews became two totally separate groups.

Paul is talking about Jews and Gentiles who have believed in Jesus, becoming one new people. We all worship God through Jesus, and we share in the one Spirit of God. All believers in Jesus can know the peace Jesus brings.

Prayer: Thank you, Lord, that Jesus gives us peace that brings people together. Amen.

For Discussion: Ask the child what he thinks peace is. Can there be different types of peace? How can we share Jesus' peace with others?

Activity: Help the child identify different situations in which some kind of peace (e.g., freedom from war, peace of mind, quietness) is involved. Talk with the child about how these different forms of peace came about. Also, identify situations where there is no peace. Use pictures, TV shows, movies and real life situations.

NOTES

Children Should Obey

Scripture: Ephesians 6:1-3

Memory: Ephesians 6:1
Children, obey your parents in the Lord, for this is right.

Memory verse for younger children:
Children, obey your parents.

Meditation: Unfortunately, obedience is a word that is losing strength and meaning in our culture, especially with children. Too often, children control their parents with manipulative devices, and the result is that the parents are often forced, in the name of peace, to obey their children. Families that recognize their rightful order in God's sight are much happier families. God intends that children are subject to God and to their parents. Children that love God will have the right attitude toward their parents. Good respect for God's order begins immediately following birth, as parents train up children in the way they should go. Properly trained children do not rule the home. When God's plan for families is in place in the home, there will be harmony, peace and proper obedience. Parents need to recognize that obedience should be the result of love and proper training, not the result of harsh, domineering parenting.

Prayer: Lord, help me to always remember to obey my parents. Amen.

For Discussion: Talk with the child about different ways the child has recently obeyed, and times when the child has not obeyed. Make sure the child knows the difference. Talk about how hard it might be to always obey. Talk with the child about how she feels when she does what her parents want her to.

Activity: Create a chart that lists the chores or regular activities the child has. Encourage the child to learn to do these things without being told. With the child, develop a system of reward for each time the child does one of the listed activities without being told. There should also be a system of deduction each time the child has to be told but does not obey. Use smaller recognition, like stars (positive) and sad faces (negative) for each event, but make sure that cumulative stars result in a larger reward.

NOTES

The Armor of God I

Scripture: Ephesians 6:10-17

Memory: Ephesians 6:11
Put on the whole armor of God, so that you may be able to stand against the wiles of the devil.

Memory verse for younger children:
Put on the whole armor of God.

Meditation: Scripture tells us (verse 12) that the struggles we have in life are not against flesh and blood, but against spiritual forces. The suit of armor is given to us to fight this spiritual battle. Each piece is significant for following Christ: the breastplate guards our hearts, to help us be faithful. The shoes of peace prepare us to share the message of peace as we go about our day. The belt of truth reminds us that Jesus is the Truth, and that truth should prevail in our lives. The helmet of salvation helps us guard our thoughts and words because we belong to Christ. The sword of the Spirit is Scripture, in which we find God's word. Learning scripture helps us not be overwhelmed by the enemy. The breastplate of faith helps us resist the methods the enemy may use to try to turn us away from Jesus' way. I put this armor on each day. In this lesson, we will think about the belt of truth, the breastplate of righteousness and the shoes of peace.

Prayer: Lord, help me to be faithful in wearing the armor so I can live as you want me to. Amen.

For Discussion: Help the child understand the significance of the breastplate, the shoes and the belt. Ask which things we use today and which might be from another time. Ask the child why he thinks God has provided this armor for us.

Activity: (1) Help the child create these armor pieces from construction paper or other materials. The pieces should be sized so that the child can wear them. (2) Find pictures of knights—or visit a museum—and help the child identify the three pieces of armor talked about in this lesson. Talk with the child about the purposes these pieces served for the knight in battle.

NOTES

The Armor of God II

Scripture: Ephesians 6:10-17

Memory: Ephesians 6:11
Put on the whole armor of God, so that you may be able to stand against the wiles of the devil.

Memory verse for younger children:
Put on the whole armor of God.

Meditation: There are Scriptures that can be matched with some of these pieces of armor: (1) the belt of truth, John 14:6; (2) the shield of faith, Proverbs 3:5 & 6; (3) the sword of the Spirit, Hebrews 4:12; and (4) the helmet of salvation, 2 Corinthians 10:5. Additionally, some of these armor pieces are mentioned in other parts of Scripture, although not necessarily as they are listed here: Isaiah 11:5 mentions two types of belts, one for the waist of righteousness, and one for the loins of truth. Isaiah 59:17 mentions putting on righteousness like a breastplate, and a helmet of salvation for the head. We may not fully understand the application of these armor pieces, but I think there is little doubt that they all serve a purpose in God's Kingdom. If we can learn to take up this armor, and remember that we bear it and put it to use in our lives, we will be much more victorious in Jesus.

Prayer: Lord, help me to be faithful in wearing the armor you have provided for my life. Amen.

For Discussion: Help the child understand the possible application of the helmet, the sword and the shield. Discuss the real-life uses of these articles in battle. While most are defensive articles, help the child see that the Sword might be used for purposes other than defense. Talk with the child about who might have these articles in real life, both in past times and modern times. What would happen if these people did not have these pieces of armor? Talk with the child about what it would be like to wear and carry all six pieces of armor. Talk a little about enemies—real and spiritual—against which armor might be used.

Activity: (1) Help the child create these three pieces of armor, in a size that can be worn or carried by the child. (2) From a visit to the museum or pictures in a book, point out these articles on a knight, asking the child how he thought they might be used.

NOTES

Winning the Race

Scripture: Philippians 3:12-14

Memory: Philippians 3:14
I press on toward the goal for the prize of the heavenly call of God in Christ Jesus.

Memory verse for younger children:
I press on toward the goal.

Meditation: The Christian life is a process. It begins when we first hear and believe the message of salvation brought by Jesus and continues throughout our life until we see Jesus face to face. Paul, in this letter to the church at Philippi, compares the process to a race, with the goal being the prize of our heavenly calling in God through Christ. Until we leave this life, we can never consider that we have arrived, but one day we will all cross the finish line, and the prize will be ours. It is an incredible prize that will be shared by many people. Part of the process is looking forward, not behind. The past has served its purpose in our lives—and we should remember those lessons—but our focus should be on what is ahead. Running this race is not easy. Many people experience times when they feel it is not worth the effort. That may be because they have not really entered the race. Once we truly begin this process, by faith, it should be the desire of our heart to complete the race in good form and to receive the prize.

Prayer: Lord, help me do my best at running my race for you. Amen.

For Discussion: Talk with the child about the athletic interests the child has. Talk about everything that must be done to participate and win in these activities: learning, training, commitment, participation, discipline and completion. Help the child learn to compare the different parts of an athletic activity with living for Jesus. How do we learn? What might the training be? Why do we have to have commitment? In what ways might we participate? How does discipline (i.e., doing things we might not want to do) fit in? What does completion involve?

Activity: Make a chart with the child, identifying all the aspects of the sports or activities they participate in: e.g., uniform, equipment, practice, coaching, listening, playing fair, playing with others, not cheating, things the child does not like, being present, winning, and rewards. Help the child identify one part of running the race for Jesus with each of the aspects of the activity listed. For example, our sports uniform might compare with the armor that we are given. Practice could relate to things like reading the bible or going to Sunday school. The more we learn to relate elements of our natural lives with elements of our spiritual lives, the better we can live both.

NOTES

Rejoice Always

Scripture: Philippians 4:4

Memory: Philippians 4:4
Rejoice in the Lord always; again I will say, Rejoice.

Memory verse for younger children:
Rejoice in the Lord always.

Meditation: To rejoice does not necessarily mean to be happy. There are many things in this life that work against our happiness but we should always, as this verse indicates, be rejoicing. We can rejoice even through the greatest difficulties. The key is in the three words that follow the command: "in the Lord." When things are going on that are not of the Lord, we can't let them overwhelm us. We are always able to look to Jesus, from whom we receive our joy. This might be a difficult concept to help a child understand, because it is difficult for many adults to understand. Jesus wants to walk with us through whatever difficulty we encounter. When sources of unhappiness rear their heads, we can turn to our ever-present partner, and find joy in knowing that he is going through our difficulties with us. We can find joy in knowing that Jesus experienced worse difficulties than we will ever face, yet he endured with joy (John 17:13). So we should walk in an attitude of joy, knowing that the one who shared our difficulties brings joy to our hearts and lives (Rom. 15:13).

Happiness can come from many things in this life, but these are all passing. An ice cream cone is eaten or melts, visits to grandma end, Christmas only comes once a year. Joy in Jesus can be ours all the time, because Jesus is always with us and walks with us through our difficulties and happy times.

 Prayer: Lord, sometimes I am sad. Help me to rejoice because you know me, you know what is happening to me and you are with me. Amen.

For Discussion: Ask the child about the things that make her happy and things that make her sad. Talk about some specific things in Jesus life that might have made him happy, and some things that made him sad. Talk about how Jesus may have felt in each case and how he could rejoice. Talk with the child about the process of believing that Jesus is with them at all times, so that when difficult things are happening, they can still rejoice. Help the child understand the difference between rejoicing in the Lord and being happy.

Activity: Help the child chart out happy times and sad times and discover which happens most in his life. Help the child create or find reminders to help him remember to rejoice always, and find rewards for him when he does so.

NOTES

Don't Worry

Scripture: Philippians 4:6-7

Memory: Philippians 4:6
Do not worry about anything, but in everything by prayer and supplication
with thanksgiving let your requests be made known to God.

Memory verse for younger children:
Do not worry.

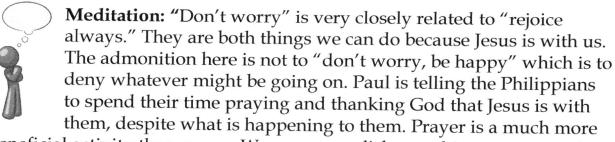

Meditation: "Don't worry" is very closely related to "rejoice always." They are both things we can do because Jesus is with us. The admonition here is not to "don't worry, be happy" which is to deny whatever might be going on. Paul is telling the Philippians to spend their time praying and thanking God that Jesus is with them, despite what is happening to them. Prayer is a much more beneficial activity than worry. Worry accomplishes nothing except maybe poor health, but prayer can do us a world of good. There is another aspect of this prayer that is important: thanking God that he has not abandoned us in our circumstances. The result of praying rather than worrying is that God's peace will guard our hearts and minds. What an incredible process and promise! When we look to God rather than to ourselves, God kicks all of God's blessings into action for our benefit.

Prayer: Dear God, thank you that I don't have to worry about things that you already know all about. Thank you for your peace. Amen.

For Discussion: Help the child discern things that worry him. Help him explore some of the reasons for his worry. *Some will be very well founded, others not so much so.* Talk about ways the child can give his worry to Jesus. Help the child find ways to pray when he is worried, no matter where he might be.

Activity: Sing the little ditty "Don't Worry, Be Happy."[2] if you know it. Help the child add and change words like "Jesus says, 'Don't Worry, Be Joyful.'" Help the child make up little songs or poems about not worrying. These can be silly or more serious, but they should come from the child. Dancing to the little tunes will help impress the message on the child.

NOTES

---

2   Don't Worry, Be Happy" is a 1988 song by musician Bobby McFerrin.

Good Things to Think About

Scripture: Philippians 4:8-9

Memory: Philippians 4:9
Keep on doing the things that you have learned and received and heard and seen in me, and the God of peace will be with you.

Memory verse for younger children:
Keep on doing the things that you have learned in me.

 **Meditation:** What kind of things do you let control your mind? TV, talk radio, movies, websites and video games are packed with things just waiting to control our thinking, if we let them. God has a better way. God says meditate—yes, meditate—on good things, things that are true, beautiful, honorable, excellent and praiseworthy. When the negative thoughts and ideas emerge, we can cancel them out by thinking of the things of God. A good daily practice might be to take these admonitions and find examples of each one each day. What will be the result? We receive that wonderful promise of peace again. God is a God of peace, and God wants to fill us with that peace, so we don't have to worry, so we can be joyful, and we can represent Jesus everywhere we go and in everything we do. We must keep our minds steadfastly on God, thinking on all the good things which God has provided in this life.

 Prayer: Dear Lord, help me to take control of my mind by thinking about all the wonderful things that you have created and provided. Amen.

For Discussion: Ask the child what he thinks about in his "spare" time. Help him discover how his thoughts might be influenced by things other than the good things of God. Discuss what might happen if the child starts thinking about good things rather than scary, hard or ugly things. Be sure to help the child discover several examples of each of the categories of this passage.

Activity: In the artistic medium which is most suited to the child, e.g., drawing or writing, encourage the child to express her feelings about the beautiful things of God's world. Help the child understand that even though they really like something, it may not necessarily be something which fits the parameters of this passage.

NOTES

Jesus Can Help Us Do Things

Scripture: Philippians 4:11-13

Memory: Philippians 4:13
I can do all things through him who strengthens me.

Memory verse for younger children:
I can do all things through him.

Meditation: Paul, who wrote the letter we call the book of Philippians to the church at Philippi, knew a secret: no matter what was going on in his life, he could find contentment in Christ, and Christ could help him do anything he needed to do and anything Christ called him to do. Regardless of his circumstances, bountiful or wanting, peaceful or stressful, he could deal with them because of the strength and power of Jesus Christ. In another place, Paul talks about being all things to all people (1 Corinthians 9:22). Paul had concerns few pastors of today know about, but he also had a source of power few pastors draw on: the power of God given through Christ and abiding in Paul in the form of the Spirit of God. Paul knew that whatever he faced in ministry to the churches he served, Christ could bring him through with contentment, peace and joy. Some think Paul has done great damage to the church of today, but when we look at this wonderfully encouraging and exhorting letter, I think we could do worse than to follow his leading.

Prayer: Thank you Lord that I can know Paul's secret and find contentment, help and peace in everything I face. Amen.

For Discussion: Talk with the child about his life, whether it is a life of plenty or a life of need. Is the child content? If not, help him learn how he might become content by trusting Jesus. Are there things which the child is facing which he feels he may not be able to do? If these are things the child currently needs to be concerned about and wants to do, help him understand that he can do whatever he has to with good effort and Jesus' help (prayer). Help him understand the importance of his own effort.

Activity: Help the child undertake a project which she might at first be uncomfortable with because of difficulty, but one which she would want to do. Plan each step, and help the child fulfill the steps one at a time. Be very patient with the child and encourage the child to be patient with herself. Make prayer an important part of each step, and help the child be content with her effort and result at each stage.

NOTES

A New Home Forever I

Scripture: Revelation 21 and 22

Memory: Revelation 21:2
And I saw the holy city, the new Jerusalem, coming down out of heaven
from God, prepared as a bride adorned for her husband.

Memory verse for younger children:
I saw the holy city coming down out of heaven.

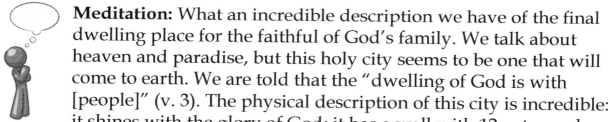

Meditation: What an incredible description we have of the final
dwelling place for the faithful of God's family. We talk about
heaven and paradise, but this holy city seems to be one that will
come to earth. We are told that the "dwelling of God is with
[people]" (v. 3). The physical description of this city is incredible:
it shines with the glory of God; it has a wall with 12 gates and
each gate is a pearl; the wall of the city was made of jasper and the city of
pure gold. There are twelve foundations and each one is made of a precious
stone. This city has no temple because the Lamb and God Almighty are
its temple. The city will have a crystal-clear river that will flow from the
throne of God. The people of this city will need no lamps, because God
will be their light. Most wonderfully, the tree of life will bear twelve crops
of fruit, one each month, and the leaves of that wondrous tree will be for
the healing of the nations. We are told that this cubic city will come from
heaven "prepared as a bride beautifully dressed for her husband." What a
beautiful description of the eternal home of God's children.

Prayer: Lord, I want to live in that beautiful city. Help me make sure that I am in right relationship with you so that I may do that. Amen.

For Discussion: Talk with the child about all the beautiful places she has seen. Read some of the physical passages about this new Holy City and talk about how they might compare with places the child has seen. Talk about how the child might get to see and go to that city. Whom does the child think she might see there? What would she do there?

Activity: In a different medium than usual, have the child depict this city. Clay, or Legos®, glitter, tiny beards and a variety of other elements might combine to present a picture of this unique city. Include in the depiction the ideas of the light, the river, the throne and the tree.

NOTES

A New Home Forever II

Scripture: Revelation 21 and 22

Memory: Revelation 21:27
But nothing unclean will enter it, nor anyone who practices abomination or falsehood, but only those who are written in the Lamb's book of life.

Memory verse for younger children:
Only those who are written in the Lamb's book of life.

Meditation: It is wonderful to meditate on the appearance of this incredible city, but the most important thing is who will be there. First of all, God and Jesus, now identified by John as the Lamb, will be there. Jesus is called the Lamb because he was sacrificed, like the lambs in the Old Testament. God and Jesus will be the temple, the place where we will worship, and they will be our light. Then, all those whose names are written in the Lamb's book of life will be there. These are those who have believed in Jesus and who have overcome anything that might have turned them away from Jesus. This is an uncountable group of people. We are told that we will drink without cost from the spring of the water of life. All of our tears will be wiped away, and there will be no more death or mourning or crying or pain. We will see the Lamb, and serve him, and his name will be on our foreheads. We will be his forever more. Jesus will welcome into this city all who washed their robes and have the right to the tree of life. We will march proudly into the gates of that city, as Jesus rode victoriously into the gates of the city of Jerusalem just prior to his death, the death and resurrection that secured this wonderful eternity for the faithful.

Prayer: Thank you, Lord, that you purchased the admission to this beautiful city for me. I look forward to being there with you. Amen.

For Discussion: Don't let the child get overwhelmed by the descriptions of the people who won't be there. Even though the child may engage in some of the "rejecting" habits which are named in these texts, if he believes in Jesus and follows Jesus, he will have nothing to fear. Help the child to understand that Jesus will forgive us of all wrong things when we believe in him and ask him to do that for us. Talk about determining to do right things with the help of Jesus, and turning away from things that might make Jesus sad.

Activity: Help the child depict what it will be like to be with Jesus all the time. What will he and Jesus do? What will he say to Jesus? Can he show what he thinks Jesus will look like according to these texts?

NOTES

Made in the USA
Lexington, KY
10 October 2017